# COLLINS COBUILD

COLLINS Birmingham U...

# ENGLISH GUIDES

## 3

# ARTICLES

Roger Berry

THE UNIVERSITY
OF BIRMINGHAM

COLLINS
COBUILD

HarperCollins*Publishers*

HarperCollins Publishers
77-85 Fulham Palace Road
London W6 8JB

COBUILD is a trademark of William Collins Sons & Co Ltd

© HarperCollins Publishers Ltd 1993
First published 1993

Reprinted 1993

10 9 8 7 6 5 4 3 2

ISBN 0 00 370561-7

Computer typeset by Tradespools Ltd, Frome, Somerset

Printed in Great Britain by HarperCollins Manufacturing, Glasgow

To Vesna and Lukie-Luke

The author would like to thank the following people: Steve Starkey for his advice on
American usage; Dave Willis for his thoughtful comments on the text; Jim Ronald for
compiling the index; Annette Capel, Lorna Heaslip, and Charlie Ranstead at
HarperCollins; and above all Stephen Bullon and Elizabeth Manning at COBUILD for
their patience in seeing this project through.

# Contents

# Foreword

The articles in English are so important for the learner of the language that we have decided to publish a whole book about them. *The* is by far the commonest word in English, and with *a* and *an* makes up 8.5% of all text. This *Guide to Articles* is one of a series of COBUILD ENGLISH GUIDES to particular areas of difficulty for learners of English.

Many other languages have articles or similar sorts of demonstratives and their meanings are very similar to their English equivalents. It is the usage which is different – when to use an article, and when a possessive; when to be sure to put an article in, and when it is more natural to leave it out. For example in titles. In French or Italian you must put a definite article in front of all titles like Professor when you use them with a name, unless you are actually talking to the person. In English you usually do not.

When questions of usage arise, the importance of the COBUILD evidence becomes clear. This evidence comes from the Bank of English, a collection of modern English speech and writing drawn from a variety of sources. The computer files of the Bank of English currently contain approximately 200 million words. The different kinds of usage can be retrieved and their importance assessed; up-to-date tendencies can be observed. All the examples in this book (there are nearly 600) come from this huge database, and this naturally occurring data gives a real authority to the statements. (Why did I write *a real authority* and not just *real authority*? Check on page 20.)

If you do not find answers to your problems with the articles in this book, or if you have any comments or suggestions about how to improve COBUILD publications, please write to me.


John Sinclair
Editor in Chief: COBUILD ENGLISH GUIDES
Professor of Modern English Language
University of Birmingham

# Introduction

## Why are articles important?

You probably realize already how important the articles are in English. Not only are they among the commonest words in English, they are often vital for successful communication. They tell you what assumptions people make about their listeners when they speak. If a stranger comes up to you on a university campus and asks 'Where's the bookstore?', they think there is only one there, and they assume you think this too. Changing one article for another, or leaving one out, can often cause misunderstanding, for example if you say 'I like English' (the language), when you mean 'I like the English' (the people).

Articles also give you structural information; they tell you that a noun is following in the sentence. For example, if someone asks 'What's that over there?' there is a big difference between answering 'Well...' and 'A well'.

So it is not true to say that articles do not affect meaning. Exercises which simply leave gaps for articles to be put in are misleading; they suggest that the 'meaning' is already there, and that articles are just an obstacle for learners. This is not so: articles can help you to make meaning clearer or to choose between meanings.

Mistakes with articles do not always cause misunderstanding, but they can let the rest of your English down. Many people who are very good at English still have problems with articles. It is normal and justifiable to be concerned about being accurate.

## Is learning how to use the articles difficult?

Of course, learning to use articles properly isn't the easiest part of English; there isn't a simple rule as there is for knowing when to use third person '-s'. Articles are not a grammatical item added after the content has been established; they are determined by meaning.

However, article usage is regular, and it can be learnt; all native speakers of English learn it. But working your way through this book isn't the only answer; you must read and listen to English whenever you can, and try to understand it. This will strengthen the insights you gain from working with this book.

There are some situations where the choice of article is mostly automatic, for example with proper nouns. But most of the time it depends on what you are trying to say, and so you need to have a deeper understanding of the rules; even with proper nouns there are some generalizations that can help you. This difference between **convention** and **creativity** is very important for article usage.

# How can this book help?

This book has been designed to help you in three ways:

**1** There are **explanations** in simple English, with as few technical terms as possible. Rules of usage are given which are not misleading, as has often been the case. There are warnings in the text, to show particular areas where some learners need to be careful; these are based on an analysis of errors. There is also information about the few differences between British and American English.

**2** There are **examples** of real English, taken from the Bank of English; these illustrate the explanations and show you how articles are really used.

**3** There are **exercises** based on the explanations which will give you practice in various areas of article use and allow you to try out what you have read. The exercises have been designed to be as varied as possible (they aren't all of the type where you have to fill in gaps) and challenging (they aren't all mechanical, and it's possible to get them wrong).

# How to use this book

This book is organised into a number of chapters and sections so that you can deal with one area at a time. So if you want to find out when to use 'a' and when to use 'an', look at Chapter 1 on the forms of the articles. Chapter 7 tells you how to use articles with proper nouns. Chapters 3 and 4 deal with what are possibly the most important areas: the creative uses of the indefinite and definite articles. At the end of most sections there is a cross-reference to the exercises which practise the section. There is an **answer key** after the exercises.

You can use this book as a course, going through the points one by one (you will probably find you are already familiar with some) and doing the exercises; or you can use it for reference, dealing with questions and problems when they occur. For this purpose, there is an **index**, which will tell you where to find:

- information on how to use articles with particular types of words, for example adjectives or the names of geographical features like deserts and so on;

- information on particular words which are mentioned in the text because they are important for article use, for example 'television';

- an explanation of a technical term, for example 'generic'.

Roger Berry
Hong Kong 1993

# Pronunciation Guide

## vowel sounds:

| | |
|---|---|
| ɑː | heart, start, calm |
| æ | act, mass, lap |
| aɪ | dive, cry, mind |
| aɪə | fire, tyre, buyer |
| aʊ | out, down, loud |
| aʊə | flour, tower, sour |
| e | met, lend, pen |
| eɪ | say, main, weight |
| eə | fair, care, wear |
| ɪ | fit, win, list |
| iː | feed, me, beat |
| ɪə | near, beard, clear |
| ɒ | lot, lost, spot |
| əʊ | note, phone, coat |
| ɔː | more, cord, claw |
| ɔɪ | boy, coin, joint |
| ʊ | could, stood, hood |
| uː | you, use, choose |
| ʊə | lure, pure, cure |
| ɜː | turn, third, word |
| ʌ | but, fund, must |
| ə | *the weak vowel in* butter, about, forgotten |
| i | *the weak vowel in* very, create |
| u | *the first weak vowel in* tuition |

## consonant sounds:

| | |
|---|---|
| b | bed, rub |
| d | done, red |
| f | fit, if |
| g | good, dog |
| h | hat |
| j | yellow |
| k | king, pick |
| l | lip, bill |
| m | mat, ram |
| n | not, tin |
| p | pay, lip |
| r | run |
| s | soon, bus |
| t | talk, bet |
| v | van, love |
| w | win |
| x | loch |
| z | zoo, buzz |
| ʃ | ship, wish |
| ʒ | measure |
| ŋ | sing |
| tʃ | cheap, witch |
| θ | thin, myth |
| ð | then, loathe |
| dʒ | joy, bridge |

Stressed syllables are indicated by an underline under the vowel symbol for the stressed syllable.

## Corpus Acknowledgements

We would like to thank those authors and publishers who kindly gave permission for copyright material to be used in the Bank of English. We would also like to thank Times Newspapers Ltd, the BBC World Service, and National Public Radio of Washington for providing valuable data.

# 1 The forms of the articles

## 1.1 The definite and indefinite articles

This book deals with two words. These are the definite article, **the,** and the indefinite article, **a** or **an.**

*The rug was stained.*
*I have an idea she had a weight problem.*

This chapter explains how these words are written and spoken; that is, the form of the words. Section 1.2 discusses the definite article in writing and speech, and section 1.3 discusses the indefinite article in writing and speech. Section 1.4 deals with the way the articles are pronounced when they are stressed.

The forms of the articles and the rules for using them are not complicated. However, you may find it difficult to recognize the articles in spoken English; this is particularly true of the indefinite article. Usually it is unstressed and so it occurs in very short syllables. You may need to become familiar with the rhythm of English in order to notice these short unstressed syllables.

## 1.2 The definite article

The definite article, **the,** has only one form in writing.

*Here are the broad problems and the broad solutions.*

There are two pronunciations:

/ðə/ which is used before consonant sounds, and
/ði/ which is used before vowel sounds.

*The same name was given to this island.* /ðə/
*The emphasis is on discipline.* /ði/

WARNING   It is the sound, not the spelling, of the next word which matters. The word 'one' has a consonant sound at the start: /wʌn/ even though there is a vowel there in writing. Some words beginning with the letter 'u' have a consonant sound /j/ first in pronunciation. For example, 'unit' is pronounced /juːnɪt/.

The following words begin with the letter 'u' but **the** is pronounced /ðə/ before them because they begin with the sound /j/.

| | | | |
|---|---|---|---|
| ubiquitous | unilateral | universe | user |
| unanimous | union | university | usual |
| unicorn | unique | uranium | utensil |
| uniform | unit | urine | uterus |
| uniformed | united | use | utility |
| uniformity | unity | useful | utilization |
| unification | universal | useless | utopian |

*The union must be well informed and well organized.* /ðə/
*...the uniforms of the staff.* /ðə/

The consonant letters 'f', 'h', 'l', 'm', 'n', 'r', 's', and 'x' are pronounced with a vowel sound at the start when they are spoken separately, as for example when they are part of an abbreviation. So when talking about the National Health Service, you might say 'the NHS' and pronounce it /ði en eɪtʃ es/.

*The NSB pays interest on your balance.* /ði/

**WARNING** Some words begin with the letter 'h' but do not have the sound /h/ in their pronunciation. The first sound in these words is a vowel. Therefore 'honest' is pronounced /ɒnɪst/. This spelling is sometimes called 'the silent h'.

The following words begin with the letter 'h' but **the** is pronounced /ði/ before them because the letter 'h' is not pronounced:

| | | | |
|---|---|---|---|
| heir | honest | honorary | honourably |
| heiress | honestly | honour | hour |
| heirloom | honesty | honourable | hourly |

*It tried to regulate the hours of work.* /ði/

See section 1.4 for information about stressed forms.

▶ Exercises 1, 3, and 4

**Note** Occasionally you may see other ways of writing the definite article: **t'**, for example 't'other' meaning 'the other', which is a dialect form; and **th'**, which is used by writers to convey a casual way of speaking, or is used in poetry.

*How could I push her outa th' way?*

## 1.3 The indefinite article

The indefinite article has two forms, both in speech and writing:

**a** pronounced /ə/
**an** pronounced /ən/.

**A** is used before consonants and **an** is used before vowels.

*He leads a busy life.*
*He won't get an answer from me.*

As with the definite article it is the pronunciation, not the spelling, which is important. **A** is used before words which begin with a consonant sound in speech even if they begin with a vowel letter in writing (see section 1.2).

*Some took him to be a universal god.*

**An** is used before words which begin with a silent 'h' (see section 1.2), and before consonants which begin with a vowel sound when they are pronounced separately, as in some abbreviations.

*I got here an hour ago.*
*...if you save with an NSB investment account.*

See section 1.4 for information about stressed forms.

Some people use **an** in front of the words 'hotel', 'historic', 'history', 'habitual', and a few other words beginning with 'h' where the first syllable is not stressed. They do not usually pronounce the 'h' when using 'an' with these words.

*She found an hotel she knew.*

However, most people use **a** with these words.

*There I checked into a hotel.*

▶ Exercises 2, 3, and 4

## 1.4 Stressed forms

Normally in speech the articles are not stressed, but sometimes it is necessary to stress them, as for example when you want to contrast them with other words. See sections 4.14 and 7.13 for information about other situations when **the** is stressed.

**The** is pronounced /ði:/ when you are emphasizing it; **a** is pronounced /eɪ/; and **an** is pronounced /æn/.

When you are talking about the articles as individual words, it is also possible to stress the basic forms described above in sections 1.2 and 1.3. For example, if a learner makes a mistake with articles, the teacher might say 'You should have said "the" /ðə/, not "a" /ə/'.

In writing, the emphatic use of an article is usually indicated by writing it in italics (for example, *the*) or within quotation marks ('the'). In something written by hand, emphatic use is indicated by underlining the article or by writing it in capitals.

You can say /ðiː/ and /eɪ/ when you are hesitating, especially when you do not know what word to use next, as in 'This is the, er, solution'.

# 2 Articles and nouns

## 2.1 Introduction

Definite and indefinite articles go only with nouns, or words that are behaving like nouns. They are therefore a kind of **determiner**.

*The town is small and undistinguished.*
*It is only a gesture.*

Not every noun has to have an article; there may be another determiner, like 'this' or 'that', 'his' or 'my', or 'some' or 'no', or there may be no article at all (sometimes called the 'zero' article).

*He stuck to this story.*
*After some weeks his efforts bore fruit.*
*Another had only bread and soup for Sunday dinner.*

There may be several words between the article and its noun.

*...for a fairly long period.*

You cannot use an article on its own; you can say 'I like the idea', but not 'I like the'.

For more information about the structure of noun groups and the combinations of articles with other determiners, see Chapter 8.

This chapter is concerned with how the type of noun affects which article you use. Nouns can be classified according to the way in which they combine with articles in the singular or the plural. The table below shows this.

|   | SINGULAR with no article | with 'a' or 'an' | with 'the' | PLURAL with no article | with 'the' |
|---|---|---|---|---|---|
| 1 | CAKE | A CAKE | THE CAKE | CAKES | THE CAKES |
| 2 | — | A BOOK | THE BOOK | BOOKS | THE BOOKS |
| 3 | MUSIC | — | THE MUSIC | — | — |
| 4 | — | — | — | TROUSERS | THE TROUSERS |
| 5 | LONDON | — | — | — | — |
| 6 | — | — | THE DANUBE | — | — |
| 7 | — | — | — | — | THE ALPS |

**WARNING** The indefinite article is never used with a noun in the plural.

The nouns in rows 5, 6 and 7 have only one possible combination with articles. These are **proper nouns,** that is, the names of places, people and things, and they are explained in Chapter 7. In this chapter we deal with the nouns in rows 1 - 4.

The largest group of nouns refer to things that can be counted. These nouns have a singular form and a plural form, like 'book' in row 2; you can say 'a book' or 'books'. These are called **count nouns.** They are dealt with in section 2.2.

In English, you cannot say 'a music' or 'musics' because music is regarded as uncountable. Nouns like 'music' (row 3) do not have a plural and are called **uncount nouns.** They are dealt with in sections 2.3 and 2.4.

Some nouns, like 'trousers' in row 4, have only a plural form; you cannot say 'a trouser'. These are called **plural nouns.** They are dealt with in section 2.5.

Nouns like 'cake' in row 1 which can be either count nouns or uncount nouns are dealt with in section 2.6. Other sections in this chapter show how, under certain circumstances, nouns can be **converted** from uncount nouns to count nouns, or vice versa.

## 2.2 Count nouns

Section 2.1 explained that count nouns are used to refer to things which can be counted, and so they have both a singular and a plural form. In the singular, you have to use them with the definite article, the indefinite article, or another determiner.

*Even that was an error.*
*The rug was stained.*

If no other determiner is appropriate, you use the indefinite article. You cannot normally use a singular count noun without a determiner.

You can use count nouns in the plural with the definite article or with no article at all, but you cannot use them with the indefinite article.

*...so she drank coffee and smoked cigarettes.*
*The firemen cut through the bars.*

Count nouns refer to things which are regarded as separate units. Most count nouns refer to things which can be seen, touched or measured, such as tables, trees, and tennis balls; nouns which refer to these things are sometimes called **concrete nouns**.

However, some count nouns refer to things which cannot be seen, touched, or measured, such as remarks, schemes, and shocks; nouns which refer to these things are sometimes called **abstract nouns**. Here is a list of some common abstract count nouns.

| | | | | |
|---|---|---|---|---|
| address | idea | month | scheme | year |
| effect | issue | plan | shock | |
| election | method | problem | suggestion | |
| hour | minute | remark | week | |

Note, however, that most abstract nouns are uncount.

▶ Exercise 1

## 2.3 Uncount nouns

Section 2.1 explained that uncount nouns do not have a plural form.

In normal situations you cannot use the indefinite article with uncount nouns. You often have no article at all, although you can have the definite article in front of the noun.

*...the smell of fresh <u>bread</u>.*
*Make sure <u>the bread</u> is quite cool.*
*...the first real flash of <u>anger</u>.*
*...<u>the anger</u> that separated me from her.*

Uncount nouns are of three main types:

● those which refer to concrete substances or materials which are not thought of as separate units, such as 'water', 'bread', and 'salt'. These are sometimes called **mass nouns**;

● those which refer to groups of objects, such as 'furniture', 'luggage', and 'machinery';

● abstract nouns like 'love', 'anger', and 'information'.

Unless they are modified or qualified (see sections 3.7 and 4.9), uncount abstract nouns referring to qualities and feelings are usually used without an article.

*<u>Love</u> had its claims.*
*It wasn't <u>true love</u>.*

Lists of common uncount nouns can be found in Collins Cobuild English Grammar, on pages 9 and 10.

► Exercise 1

## 2.4 Uncount nouns whose equivalents in other languages are count nouns

Some uncount nouns in English have equivalents in other European languages which are count nouns or plural nouns; speakers of those languages may have to be careful when using the words in the list below. These nouns do not have a plural and cannot be used with the indefinite article. You cannot say 'She gave me a good advice' or 'I bought a furniture'.

Here is a list of words of this kind.

| | | | |
|---|---|---|---|
| advice* | health | money | traffic |
| baggage* | homework* | music* | travel |
| behaviour | information* | news* | wealth |
| equipment* | knowledge* | progress | weather |
| furniture* | luggage* | research* | |
| hair* | machinery* | shopping | |

Note that 'hair' can be used as a count noun, as in 'a hair', but it is usually used as an uncount noun to refer to all the hairs on a person's head. For example, you say 'My hair needs washing'. You do not say 'My hairs need washing'.

Here are some examples using these words.

*It was on the advice of the librarians that we both depended.*
*I've just bought some new furniture.*
*You pay the rest of the money when you complete.*
*...offering music as good as most in London.*
*...congested with traffic.*

You can use expressions such as 'a piece of', 'a bit of', or 'an item of' with the words marked with an asterisk * in the above list, to refer to one individual thing. See section 2.11.

*What he saw was a piece of furniture.*

► Exercise 1

## 2.5 Plural nouns

Nouns like 'trousers' which only occur in the plural form behave like uncount nouns with regard to articles. They can have the definite article or no article at all in front of them.

*...all the goods lost in the fire.*
*...a rather sober-looking gentleman in a black coat and striped trousers.*
*We may have cause to give thanks.*

You cannot talk about 'a good' or 'a trouser'. Also, you cannot use numbers with these nouns; it is not possible to say 'ten clothes'. Here is a list of common plural nouns.

| | | | |
|---|---|---|---|
| arms* | effects* | particulars | stalls* |
| clothes | funds* | premises* | surroundings |
| congratulations | goods | regards* | thanks |
| contents | looks* | remains | troops* |
| customs* | odds | savings* | wages |
| earnings | papers* | spirits* | |

Those marked with an asterisk can be used in the singular, but the meaning is different; for example, 'arms' are weapons, but 'an arm' is a part of the body.

Some plural nouns refer to items of clothing and other objects consisting of two parts. Here is a list of plural nouns of this kind.

| | | | | |
|---|---|---|---|---|
| binoculars | knickers | pyjamas | spectacles | tweezers |
| glasses | leggings | scissors | tights | |
| jeans | pants | shorts | trousers | |

You can show that you are talking about one item by using 'a pair of'.

*He would like to have a pair of scissors.*
*You can make do with a pair of jeans.*
*He held up a pair of glasses.*

Some nouns, like 'news', 'economics', 'mathematics', and 'physics', look as if they are plural but in fact are uncount nouns, and are followed by a singular verb form. For example, you say 'The news is bad', not 'The news are bad'.

► Exercise 2

## 2.6 Nouns which can be count or uncount

The table in 2.1 shows that there are nouns like 'cake' which can be count nouns or uncount nouns. When using these nouns, you can either consider the thing you are talking about as a substance, or as an individual object. If you consider it a substance, you use an uncount noun: 'cake'; if you consider it an object, you use a count noun: 'a cake'.

*We had cake for supper.*
*The flavour of a Christmas cake will be greatly improved if the cake is sprinkled with rum or brandy before storing.*

Here is a list of words of this kind.

| | | | | |
|---|---|---|---|---|
| bone | cord | muscle | rock | toffee |
| cabbage | egg | onion | rope | wire |
| cake | fish | pie | stew | |
| chicken | fog | powder | stone | |
| chocolate | fruit | pudding | string | |
| cloud | lettuce | ribbon | thread | |

The following abstract nouns also behave like this because they can refer to a state or process in general or to an instance of it.

| | | | |
|---|---|---|---|
| ambition | divorce | marriage | retreat |
| analysis | doubt | meaning | sound |
| attack | escape | murder | suicide |
| change | failure | noise | suspicion |
| conflict | famine | opportunity | theft |
| controversy | fear | pain | victory |
| death | hope | pregnancy | war |
| desire | improvement | protest | |
| difficulty | investment | rebellion | |
| disagreement | life | recession | |

*Never use a natural fibre such as string.*
*Tie a string around it.*

*...as cold as stone.*
*There is a centre stone.*

*They ran into difficulty.*
*This is not a difficulty which will quickly disappear.*

*It was the first time in my ten years of marriage that I had gone out alone at night.*
*...a marriage which was superficially a failure.*

*...to put the issue beyond doubt.*
*...without a shadow of a doubt.*

In other cases where a noun can be both count and uncount there is a small but predictable difference in meaning. Nouns which are usually uncount nouns can be converted to count nouns when:

- they refer to a unit of something (see section 2.7)
- they mean a type of something (see section 2.8)

Nouns which are usually count nouns can be used as uncount nouns after expressions such as 'a type of', 'a kind of', 'a sort of', 'a variety of', and so on (see section 2.9).

In still other cases, there is no connection, or only a distant one, between an uncount noun and the same word used as a count noun, such as between 'paper' and 'a paper'. For more information on words like this see 2.10.

▶ Exercise 4

## 2.7 Converting uncount nouns to count nouns meaning 'a unit of'

Many mass nouns (see section 2.3) can become count nouns when they are used to refer to an amount of something in a container. So if you are offering someone a drink of coffee in a cup or a mug, you can say 'Would you like a coffee?'

*He ordered a coffee.*

Compare this with a general statement:

*Coffee and tea are not good drinks for children.*

For different drinks and substances there are different accepted units and containers. For 'sugar' it is a lump or spoonful; for 'whisky' the usual container is a glass but the quantity varies. So if someone says to you 'Give me a whisky', they mean a small glass, not a bottle. 'A beer' can mean a glass, can, or bottle of beer.

*Will you have a whisky, Doctor?*
*Want a beer?*

Here is a list of words which are frequently used in this way.

| | | | |
|---|---|---|---|
| beer | Coke | rum | vodka |
| brandy | gin | sherry | whisky |
| coffee | lager | sugar | yoghurt |

Note that some other words are used like this in restaurants and cafes but not in people's homes. For example, you might ask for 'two teas' in a cafe, but someone in their own home would probably say 'Would you like some tea?' or 'Would you like a cup of tea?' rather than 'Would you like a tea?'

▶ Exercises 3 and 4

## 2.8 Converting uncount nouns to count nouns meaning 'a type of'

You can also convert an uncount noun to a count noun when you mean 'a type of' or 'a variety of' something. For example, 'cheese' is a general word for that particular food and 'a cheese' is a variety or kind of cheese, just as 'wine' is the general word and 'a wine' is a variety of wine.

*...a wine of the region.*
*I was impressed by a wine from Friuli.*
*Supper consisted of onion soup, black sausage with tomato salad, and a local cheese with herbs.*
*When boiled to setting point with an equal weight of sugar, they make a very fine jam.*

Here is a list of words which are frequently used in this way.

| | | | |
|---|---|---|---|
| beer | jam | paint | whisky |
| brandy | lager | perfume | wine |
| cheese | meat | sauce | wood |
| coffee | medicine | soup | |
| detergent | metal | tea | |

Note that some words, such as 'coffee', 'beer', and 'whisky' can be used as count nouns to mean either 'a unit of' or 'a type of'.

▶ Exercises 3, 4, and 5

## 2.9 Converting count nouns to uncount nouns

Count nouns can be converted to uncount nouns when they are preceded by expressions like 'a type of', 'a kind of', 'a sort of', 'a variety of', or 'a breed of'. These expressions are followed by a noun with no article, so you say 'a type of cigarette' not 'a type of a cigarette'.

*...a certain type of player.*
*...a sort of tower.*
*...a kind of dance.*
*...an exotic breed of dog.*

Note that after plural expressions like 'types of' and 'kinds of', you can use either the plural form of a noun or the noun with no article: 'different types of chemicals' or 'different types of chemical'.

Occasionally, conversion of this kind can also happen after expressions like 'a piece of' and 'a bit of' when you are referring to something that you are regarding on this occasion as a substance, although it is normally regarded as an object.

*Another child proffered a piece of biscuit.*
*She took a piece of beefburger from his plate.*

▶ Exercise 6


## 2.10 Nouns which can be count or uncount with different meanings

There is a large group of nouns in English which can be either count or uncount but which have different meanings when they are different kinds of nouns.

*...the cost of paper.*
*...the costs of producing a paper.*

In the first example 'paper' is an uncount noun and refers to the substance we write or print on; in the second example it is a count noun and means 'a newspaper'. We are not talking about conversion as described above in sections 2.7, 2.8, and 2.9; here you cannot predict the difference in meaning. The relationship between 'paper' and 'a paper' is not the same as between 'cheese' and 'a cheese' or 'coffee' and 'a coffee'.

Here are some common words which behave like this.

| | | | |
|---|---|---|---|
| accommodation | experience | law | speech |
| air | faith | light | study |
| beauty | game | memory | talk |
| business | glass | paper | time |
| charity | grammar | play | tin |
| charm | history | reason | trust |
| cold | iron | room | wood |
| dinner | language | rubber | work |
| education | lamb | space | youth |

'A wood' is not a quantity of the substance wood, or a type of wood; it is a large group of trees growing together. Here are some more examples:

*...a long building of iron and glass.*
*He filled a glass and drank it down.*

*...to give the students practical experience.*
*...a very remarkable experience.*

*You have to rely on <u>reason</u>, not authority.*
*A <u>reason</u> must exist for the KGB's intervention.*

*It was pleasant <u>work</u>.*
*That, to me, is not <u>a work</u> of art.*

▶ Exercises 7 and 8

## 2.11 Using counting expressions such as 'a piece of' and 'a bit of' with uncount nouns

Some uncount nouns, such as 'information', 'chalk', and 'clothing', cannot be converted to count nouns. However, with many uncount nouns, it is possible to refer to a particular item by using an expression such as 'a piece of' before the noun.

*...<u>a piece of</u> information that hardly surprised him.*

Other common expressions used like this are 'a bit of', which suggests a small amount, and 'an item of', which is used particularly with abstract nouns like 'advice', 'information', 'news' and so on.

*...dangling from <u>a bit of</u> bent wire.*
*...<u>an expensive item of</u> equipment.*

With some uncount nouns, you use expressions which have a more restricted meaning or use. For example, you can say 'a loaf of bread', 'a slice of bread' and 'a crumb of bread'; 'a lump of sugar' and 'a spoonful of sugar'; 'a grain of sand' and 'a grain of rice'; 'a drop of water' and 'a drop of ink'; 'a bar of soap' and 'a bar of chocolate'; 'an article of clothing' and 'an item of clothing'.

*She found <u>a loaf of bread</u> and some butter.*
*...chewing at <u>a lump of sugar</u>.*
*...quarrelling over <u>a grain of corn</u>.*
*Everyone was issued with <u>a bar of soap</u>.*

A number of count nouns are related closely in meaning (and sometimes in form) to uncount nouns; for example, 'a laugh' (count) is related to 'laughter' (uncount) in both meaning and form. While the uncount noun refers to something in general, the count noun can be used to refer to one or more items or instances of it.

*...a good deal of nervous <u>laughter</u>.*
*'Look!' one boy shouted with <u>a</u> loud <u>laugh</u>.*
*The commentary on the boat raised <u>a</u> few <u>laughs</u>.*

Here are some pairs of words like this.

| | | |
|---|---|---|
| laughter - a laugh | poetry - a poem | trouble - a problem |
| luggage - a suitcase/bag | play* - a game | |
| machinery - a machine | room* - a space | |

The words marked with an asterisk can be used as count nouns, but when they are, their meaning is not closely related to their meaning as uncount nouns.

▶ Exercises 4 and 9

# 3 Using the indefinite article

## 3.1 Introduction

This chapter explains how to use the indefinite article, **a** or **an**. The easiest way to think of the indefinite article is to regard it as the basic member of the article system and to use it, with singular count nouns, when there is no reason for using the definite article or another determiner. Chapter 2 explained how you can decide whether a noun is a count noun or not. Chapter 4 explains when you should use the definite article.

Only the main uses of the indefinite article are dealt with in this chapter. For information about how the indefinite article is used to make generic statements such as 'A rabbit needs to spend much of its time eating', see Chapter 5, section 5.2. For information about how the indefinite article is used with proper nouns, see Chapter 7, sections 7.13 and 7.14.

## 3.2 Using the indefinite article to introduce something

You usually use the indefinite article when you are introducing a particular thing (or person) into a conversation or text for the first time and you cannot assume that your listener or reader knows which particular thing you are talking about. (But see section 4.13.)

*After weeks of looking, we eventually bought a house.*
*I've been reading an interesting article in The Economist.*
*When he went to bed, he put a bag of salt beside his head.*
*Recently the TUC put forward a plan for national recovery.*

Note that if you can assume that people will know what you are talking about, then you usually introduce the thing using the definite article. See Chapter 4, especially sections 4.2, 4.3, and 4.4, for a comparison of **a** with **the** when introducing something new.

The most important point, then, is that you use the indefinite article when people do not yet know what you are referring to. Later on, if you want to refer to the thing (or person) again, you can in some cases repeat the noun with the definite article, although more often you use a personal pronoun such as 'it', 'he', 'him', 'she', or 'her'.

*...if I could find a nice girl and marry her.*

With plural count nouns you can have no determiner; when you want to refer back, you can use the same noun with the definite article, or the pronouns 'they' and 'them'.

*Ministers stress privately that they are determined to continue negotiations.*

▶ Exercise 1

## 3.3 Referring to any thing or person of a particular type

You also use the indefinite article when you are not referring to a particular thing or person, but just to any thing or person of a particular type.

*I had never owned a pet otter.*

This use is typical after verbs like 'want', 'look for', and 'need', and in questions and negatives.

*Look, the dogs want a ride.*
*Daisy refused to look for a job.*
*We need a leader urgently.*
*Have you got a book that would tell me what to do?*
*I can't afford a car.*

The difference between this use and the use described in section 3.2 is that here you are not talking about a particular thing, so you cannot refer back to it with 'it', 'he', 'she', etc. If you want to refer again to the same sort of thing you still use the indefinite article, or more likely the pronoun 'one'.

*I have never had a dog since Jonnie; I have not wanted one.*
*A barrel top would be ideal, I thought, if I could manage to find one intact.*
*Get me a car. I want a car.*

With plural count nouns you can have no determiner.

*We want answers.*
*They all need shoes now, but they have to wait until I can afford some.*

▶ Exercise 1

## 3.4 Using the indefinite article to describe things and people

You use the indefinite article not only to introduce something but to describe or give information about something that has already been introduced. This use is common with verbs like 'be', 'seem', 'look', or 'sound', or where the description immediately follows the noun.

*He is after all a widely-published scholar, an expert in his field.*
*It is a frightful place.*
*This seemed a logical approach.*
*You look an idiot.*
*...Callahan, a trim, energetic bachelor.*

You also use the indefinite article when you are saying what someone's job or profession is. This is different from some European languages, which do not use the indefinite article in this situation. In English, you have to say 'He is a teacher'. You do not say 'He is teacher'. (But see section 6.14.)

*...Richard Leech, who was a doctor.*
*Mr Stanley Boden, aged 46, a school teacher, is the Labour candidate.*

▶ Exercise 2


## 3.5 The indefinite article and 'one'

It is sometimes said that the indefinite article is really a weak form of the number 'one'. There is a little truth in this, because historically the indefinite article has developed from the number, and it sometimes still behaves like 'one'. However, in most cases it is not possible to replace the indefinite article with 'one'; the result would be very strange English. You can say 'You look an idiot', but you could not possibly say 'You look one idiot'. In the same way you can say 'It's a frightful place', but you would not say 'It's one frightful place'. So if you have no indefinite article in your language, it does not usually help to think of it as another way of saying 'one'.

However, there are situations where the indefinite article clearly has an idea of 'one', in particular in the numbers 'a hundred', 'a thousand', 'a million', 'a dozen', and so on, when they are alone or followed by a noun.

*Johnny has at least fifty, worth over a hundred dollars each.*
*It lasted a thousand years.*

In these examples you could replace **a** with 'one' with little difference in meaning, although 'one' is more emphatic. This is also true of words which refer to standard measurements.

*...seemed more like an hour.*

*I owe it all to a pound of dog meat.*
*He poured an inch of beer into my glass.*

Note the following points:

● When numbers are written as figures, the indefinite article is not included, so you write '100', '1000', but you say: 'a hundred', 'a thousand' or 'one hundred', 'one thousand'. When the figure 1 refers to 100 but is not the first part of the number, then you must say it as 'one': '2100' must be said as 'two thousand, one hundred'. Again, when saying a number between 1100 and 1999, you say 'one', not 'a': '1400' must be said as 'one thousand, four hundred'.

● You cannot use 'one' for emphasis in idiomatic expressions such as 'ninety-nine times out of a hundred' (ie 'nearly always') and 'a thousand times' (ie 'very many times'). These expressions are fixed.

● 'One' must be used when using two words referring to measurements, for example 'foot' and 'inch': 'It's one foot ten inches long'. When using just one word referring to a measurement, you use a unless you want to show you are being precise: 'It's a foot long'.

● Both the indefinite article and 'one' can be used with most fractions, but the indefinite article is more usual: 'a tenth' or 'one tenth,' 'a quarter' or 'one quarter'. 'One' is rarely used with 'half', and in an expression like 'half an hour', 'one' is not possible. See Chapter 8, section 8.4 for information about 'half'.

As stated above in section 3.2, you normally use a, not 'one', when mentioning something for the first time. 'One' is only used before nouns in the following ways:

● when being precise or emphasizing that only one thing is involved

*I have two younger brothers and one sister.*
*I've only got one room, but there's a couch.*
*One look at Mopani clearly showed him that such an approach would not do.*
*She was hopping on one foot.*

Note that 'one more' is an emphatic way of saying 'another'.

*I think he should be given one more chance.*

● when contrasting one thing in a pair or a group with another

*I went off with a bottle under one arm and some extra diapers under the other.*

Note that 'one' can be used as a pronoun in a noun group beginning with the indefinite article. The noun group must have an adjective in it. You use a noun group like this when referring to something of the same kind as what you have just been talking about.

*'The cage is too small.' - 'We're going to make a bigger one.'*

▶ Exercise 3

## 3.6 Using the indefinite article to express rates

The indefinite article is used between two noun groups to express a rate or ratio. You can talk about prices, salaries, and speeds in this way.

*...as fast as 500 kilometres an hour.*
*...rising by 1 per cent a year.*
*...a thousand pounds a week.*
*She worked 14 hours a day.*

This construction can also express the frequency with which something happens, using 'once', 'twice', 'three times', and so on.

*Kate visited him daily, sometimes twice a day.*

You can express a similar idea more emphatically with 'each' or 'every'. In more formal or technical contexts, 'per' is often used.

*Approximately 10 per cent of households move each year.*
*...twenty or thirty times every second.*
*At the end of 1973 membership fees were raised to 25p per month per head (three pounds per year).*

Note that it is also possible to use **the** in rates denoting prices, but this is very rare.

*Petrol costs around three pounds the gallon.*

▶ Exercise 4

## 3.7 Using the indefinite article with abstract uncount nouns

Many abstract uncount nouns, that is, nouns referring to things which cannot be seen, touched or measured, can be used with the indefinite article when an adjective is used with them. For example, if you talk about 'a sudden violent hatred', you mean a particular kind of hatred which is sudden and violent.

## Using the indefinite article with abstract uncount nouns

...*a passionate hatred of feminists*.
...*working up a passing anger*.
...*a certain quaint charm*.

Compare this with their use as uncount nouns when there are no adjectives.

*How long can hatred last?*
...*in a voice choked with anger.*
*He had neither charm nor humour.*

You don't have to use the indefinite article with such nouns just because of the adjectives; you can still use them without an article if you don't want to emphasize their individual, particular nature.

...*a man of immense personal charm.*

Instead of adjectives before the noun, you can have some form of qualification after it, for example a clause beginning with 'that'.

...*a charm that contains heavy doses of boyishness.*

# 4 Specific uses of the definite article

## 4.1 Introduction: different uses of the definite article

The most important part of using the articles is to know when to use the definite article, **the**. Most errors with articles made by learners of English involve the definite article.

There are times when you must use the definite article because of the noun that follows, for example with some proper nouns (Chapter 7) and some nouns referring to systems or institutions (Chapter 6). But usually it is up to speakers or writers to decide whether to use the definite article (instead of the indefinite article or no article, or another determiner) in front of a noun. This decision depends on the kind of information that they want to give their listeners or readers.

The basic question is: what are you referring to? If you are referring to a whole class or species of something we call this **generic** reference.

*The Russians are no less perceptive.*

Here we mean Russians in general. There are a number of ways of using articles for generic reference and they are dealt with in Chapter 5.

In this chapter we are concerned with another type of reference, **specific reference**, where you are specifically referring to a particular thing, person, or group, as in the example below.

*The Russians stood on their chairs to get a better view.*

**Specific reference** is much more common than **generic reference**.

## 4.2 Referring to a particular thing using the definite article or indefinite article

You can use the definite or the indefinite article (or another determiner) when you are referring to a particular thing using a singular count noun.

*Has the reporter for the Post left yet?*
*I'm taking you to a hotel.*

(When using a plural count noun or an uncount noun, you can use the definite article or another determiner, or have no article.)

Knowing when to use **the** and when to use **a** or **an** in this situation is very important. Basically, you use **the** when you think your listener will be able to identify the thing you are referring to, whether or not it has been explicitly referred to before. Otherwise, you use **a** or **an** (if you are referring to one thing using a count noun).

So when you use **the** you imply to your listener that you are referring to an **identifiable** thing, person, or group.

*Why didn't they all follow him into the living-room?*

**WARNING** One thing that is often said is that the first time you mention something you use **a** or **an,** and the second time you use **the.** This is only occasionally true; as you will see below in sections 4.4 onwards, people do not usually use **the** and the same noun when referring back to something they mentioned before.

There are three sorts of information which listeners and readers can use to work out why the definite article has been used and to identify what items are being talked about. These are:

1) what has been said earlier in a conversation or text. This process is sometimes called **referring back** or **anaphora**.

*But it seemed Mrs Colombo owned a dog which her youngest son adored. The landlord had received complaints about the dog barking at night.*

These uses are described in sections 4.3, 4.4, and 4.5.

2) the context or situation in which you are speaking or writing.

*Of course the children interrupt you, and so does the milkman.* (someone is talking about their home life)

Obviously the situation is much clearer when you are speaking with someone face-to-face, and so this use is particularly important in speech. These **situational** uses of the definite article are dealt with in sections 4.6, 4.7, and 4.8.

3) the language that you use with the noun, as part of the noun group.

*We look at it in a bit more detail at the end of the chapter.*

These uses are dealt with in sections 4.9, 4.10, and 4.11.

Don't forget that there are other determiners which give more precise information than **the** and which have to be used sometimes in cases where you might expect something to be identifiable simply with **the**. For example, you generally use a possessive determiner when referring to part of someone's body, someone's relatives, and someone's personal possessions; you would say 'Sarah's hurt her arm' or 'John's lost his wallet', not 'Sarah's hurt the arm' or 'John's lost the wallet'. (But see section 6.13.) And you generally use the determiners 'this' and 'that' when drawing attention to something; for example, you would say 'I hate living in this flat', not 'I hate living in the flat'.

▶ Exercise 1

## 4.3 Referring back to something mentioned before

If something has been introduced and established in a conversation or text (perhaps using the indefinite article), it is possible to refer to it again using the same noun with the definite article.

*But then I came on a man playing a harp. It was a black harp...and the man was dressed as a gorilla!*

This is the type of use of **the** that most books for learners concentrate on, but it is not very common, for one simple reason: if it is clear what item you are referring back to, you normally use a pronoun.

*Just then he smelled a dog and heard it curiously sniffing.*

Some books give examples like 'I have bought a book. The book cost £2.50'. This is very strange English because you would normally say 'It cost...' or '...which cost...'.

Sometimes, however, you may need to repeat the noun with the definite article:

● when the first mention occurred a long time before and a pronoun would not make a connection with it, as in the example above with 'a man - the man'

● when you are referring to one of two different people or things that have just been mentioned together

*Suddenly Marsha heard what sounded like a fight between a man and a woman. She tensed, prepared to call help, till she realised that the woman seemed to be getting the better of it.*

● when you want to add something to the noun

*The full development of an idea may well take years of hard work but the idea itself may arrive in a flash of insight.*

● as a way of avoiding repeating a pronoun too often.

*Pouncing on an idea as soon as it appears kills the idea.*
*Lyn lived with her husband in a house that they had bought for a song in nearby Seyer Street. The house was cheap partly because it was falling down.*

▶ Exercises 1 and 2

## 4.4 Something mentioned before: using another noun

When you are referring back to something, you don't have to repeat the same noun or use a pronoun; you can also use another, more general, noun.

*The civilizing influence in my first home was a small puppy which swiftly grew to the size of a small sofa. By the time the dog had chewed her way around for a week...*
*There was an enormous cat crouching on the counter...The animal looked up at Mrs Bixby.*

In speech and informal writing, 'thing' and 'place' are often used in this way.

*Angelica took the shell in both her hands and we peered at the thing.*
*He had a congenital dislike of France and everything to do with the place.*

This use is common when you want to add an adjective as a comment.

*The horse just threw me off, lay down and kicked its legs in the air. I had to remount the wretched animal at once.*

If you used the indefinite article with the more general noun, you would be introducing another item. Consider the following sentence:

*He was trying to warn that there was a leopard about and to say that all night long he had been threatened by the animal.*

'The animal' refers back to 'a leopard'. If the phrase was 'an animal', it would refer to an animal which was probably not the leopard.

▶ Exercise 3

## 4.5 Things associated with a previous mention

If you want to talk about something that is associated with an earlier item (even though you haven't mentioned it before) you can

# Specific uses of the definite article

use the definite article to show that there is a relationship or association between the items.

*I went to the window again to try to smash <u>the glass.</u>*
*He needed a whisky, but <u>the bottle</u> was empty.*
*She extended an arm, <u>the hand</u> full of grapes.*
*Then I saw a car parked by the side of the road. <u>The driver</u> was asleep.*

Here the examples are referring to the glass in the window, the bottle containing the whisky, and so on, and the definite article provides this information. The writer need not have mentioned the glass and the bottle before; the meaning is clear because the writer and reader share the knowledge that windows are made of glass, and that whisky is sold in bottles.

You can use abstract as well as concrete nouns in this way.

*He occasionally sold a picture by reducing <u>the price.</u>*

Anything associated with a previous noun can be mentioned using the definite article, so long as you think your listener or reader shares your associations.

It is not only a noun that can start this kind of association. A verb expressing an action can have the same effect.

*When you employ the best you pay. Half a million dollars is <u>the price.</u>*
*You live in Paris. <u>The address</u> is in your passport.*

The price for what? For employing the best. And which address? The address where he lives in Paris.

On the opposite page are lists of items that could be associated with the topics 'a book' and 'a cruise': note that plural count nouns and uncount nouns are included, as well as singular count nouns. Some items will depend on the type of book or voyage.

If there are several or many things of a particular type associated with your topic, you cannot usually refer to one of them by using **the.** You can use 'one of the' or, sometimes, the indefinite article. For example, when talking about a cruise, you would not say 'the passenger'; you would say 'one of the passengers' or 'a passenger'.

However, if you use the indefinite article when referring to something of which there is only one associated with your topic, you suggest that there is no close association between the item you are mentioning and your topic. For example, if you were talking about a cruise and then said, 'I sat watching a ship in the harbour', you would be implying that the ship was not the ship you were making the cruise on.

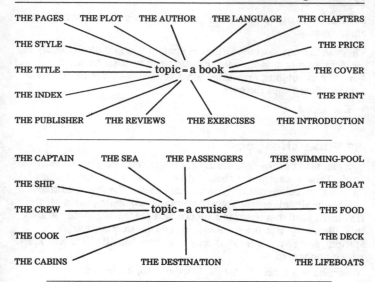

THE PAGES   THE PLOT   THE AUTHOR   THE LANGUAGE   THE CHAPTERS
THE STYLE                                            THE PRICE
THE TITLE            topic = a book                  THE COVER
THE INDEX                                            THE PRINT
THE PUBLISHER   THE REVIEWS   THE EXERCISES   THE INTRODUCTION

THE CAPTAIN   THE SEA   THE PASSENGERS   THE SWIMMING-POOL
THE SHIP                                            THE BOAT
THE CREW            topic = a cruise                THE FOOD
THE COOK                                            THE DECK
THE CABINS         THE DESTINATION        THE LIFEBOATS

▶ Exercises 4 and 5

## 4.6 Surrounding situation

We saw in section 4.5 one case where you need not mention an item
first before using the definite article, provided that there is an
association with a previously mentioned item. However, even this
is not necessary if the place or situation you are in makes it clear
what you are talking about. If you are in a garden, it is possible to
talk about 'the roses' straight away without mentioning them first
as 'roses' or 'some roses'. Indeed, if in a garden you talk about
'roses' without the definite article your listener will assume that
you are not talking about the particular ones there.

*'I can only apologize for <u>the roses</u>. The whole lot should be pulled
out.'*
*'Pass <u>the salt.</u>'*
*'Where's <u>the phone</u>?'*
*'It's on <u>the desk.</u>'*

You can only use the definite article in this way to refer to things
that you and your listener expect to find in the situation. In a
kitchen, for example, you could ask 'Where's the salt?', but it would

27

be unusual to say 'Where's the chalk?' unless you regularly keep chalk there.

This use is limited to the situation around you and so obviously is mostly found in speech, but it can occur in writing where the situation is obvious; for example, you might see a notice on a gate saying 'Please shut the gate'.

▶ Exercise 6

## 4.7 Wider situations

You can also use the definite article when you and your listener (or reader) share knowledge about things outside your surroundings. So in a particular country you can talk about 'the Prime Minister' or 'the President' or 'the Queen' without mentioning them before, if you are sure that there is only one and that your listener knows this. Similarly, in a town you could refer to 'the hospital', 'the station', and so on, if there is only one, or if your listener will know which one you mean.

*'Where have you been?' - 'At the hospital with our maid.'*
*I've got to collect my husband from the station.*
*Which reminds me! I wanted to slip up to the shop for a packet of biscuits.*

Wider situation is just an extension of surrounding situation; there is no exact dividing line. But while surrounding situations (section 4.6) are changing all the time, wider situations are fairly fixed. We each have many of them: the street, the neighbourhood, the district, the region, the country, and so on. And while the surrounding situation is clear to speakers and listeners, sometimes it may not be clear which wider situation is relevant. So if an Englishman mentions 'the Prime Minister' when he is staying in Poland, it may not be clear whether he means the Prime Minister of the United Kingdom or the Prime Minister of Poland.

▶ Exercise 7

## 4.8 Referring to unique items

There are several things which are said to be **unique** in that only one example of them (or one set of them) exists. This is an obvious case for using the definite article.

*And we're one of the most generous nations in the world.*
*After a while the sun gets warmer.*
*...when the stars fall from the sky.*
*...with the moon shining in darkness.*

Here are some words which belong to this group.

| the devil | the north pole | the solar system | the universe |
|-----------|----------------|------------------|--------------|
| the earth | the planets | the south pole | the weather |
| the equator | the pope | the stars | the world |
| the moon | the sky | the sun | |

In some ways unique nouns are like proper nouns (see Chapter 7) which also typically refer to only one item or set of items. And there is a tendency to use a capital letter with some of them (especially 'devil', 'earth', 'equator', 'north pole', 'south pole' and 'pope'), as with proper nouns.

*...a human being possessed by the Devil.*
*...on the surface of the Earth.*

However, it is not true to say that all these nouns only occur with the definite article. You can use most of them (but not 'earth' or 'weather') with the indefinite article or as plurals. If you talk of 'a sun' or 'a moon', you may be talking about another sun or moon elsewhere in the universe, or you may be trying to give a particular impression of ours.

*...under a still-warm October sun.*
*The moons, too, rapidly grew larger.*

And 'earth' is very often used without an article, especially after 'on'.

*...the smallest nation on earth.*

In reality, unique nouns are an extreme case of the situational uses described above in sections 4.6 and 4.7. Here the 'situation' is so large that it includes almost all of our experience; but it is still possible to go beyond it in space and time. There is only one pope at the moment but in the past there have been many popes. When we say 'the sun', the situation is our solar system, but of course there are other suns elsewhere in the universe.

Other nouns which can be considered as referring to unique items are nouns referring to directions, and nouns referring to specific periods of time. These are dealt with in sections 6.9 and 6.10.

▶ Exercise 8

## 4.9 Nouns with qualification

The definite article is also used with nouns when it is the phrase or
clause following the noun (rather than a previous word or the
general situation) which indicates which thing the noun refers to.
Nouns with phrases or clauses after them are said to be **qualified**.

*It is the title of the chapter.*
*...haunted by the fear that no one would turn up.*

Nouns can be qualified in a number of ways:

● by prepositional phrases:

*The only way to learn the price of something is to pay for it.*
*The reason for this selection is obvious.*
*...on the basis of the data in Table 7.1.*
*Of course he knew the answer to that one.*

The preposition most commonly used in these phrases is 'of': see
section 4.10.

● by relative clauses:

*What about the argument that reality isn't like that?*
*...the amount it cost to build the house.*
*...to get back to the hotel where he was staying.*
*...the success which has been achieved.*

● by clauses with non-finite verbs (that is, infinitives or
participles):

*Power at work is the power to get decisions implemented.*
*...the interest paid on overdrafts and credit cards.*

● by apposition (using one noun group to qualify another)

*And he wrote a book with the title 'The Summing Up'.*

Note that when uncount nouns referring to qualities or feelings are
used with **the,** it is usually because they are qualified.

*I tried to concentrate on the beauty of the scenery.*
*I share the anger that many of you must feel.*

(For a more detailed discussion of qualification, see Collins
Cobuild English Grammar, pages 128-135.)

▶ Exercise 9

## 4.10 Nouns qualified by an 'of'-phrase

There are two cases where an 'of'-phrase after a noun suggests a
unique interpretation and so normally requires the definite article.

Firstly, where the noun involved refers to an action, event, or state and the 'of'-phrase indicates the performer of the action or the thing affected:

*...following the closure of a Courtaulds factory.*
*Orders should not be cashed after the death of the person.*
*...the elimination of low pay.*

Here the first nouns refer to (possible) actions or events, and can be related to verbs: a factory was closed, the person died, low pay was or will be eliminated.

Secondly, certain nouns which refer to a part or characteristic of something are followed by an 'of'-phrase very frequently, and have unique reference.

*...after the beginning of the tax year.*
*The price of copper fell spectacularly.*
*...Picture 5 at the top of page 43.*
*...at the end of 1980.*

The tax year has only one beginning, copper has only one price, page 43 has only one top, 1980 has only one end. Here are some nouns like this.

| | | | |
|---|---|---|---|
| back | end | middle | top |
| beginning | front | price | weight |
| bottom | height | size | |
| edge | length | title | |

Note that you can also use the definite article before these nouns even when they are not qualified because they are often found in association with other nouns which have been mentioned before (see section 4.5).

▶ Exercises 9 and 10

## 4.11 Superlative adjectives

Superlative adjectives tend to occur with the definite article, for example, 'the tallest', 'the cleverest', 'the fastest'. This is because they refer to the item (or set of items) in a group which is extreme with regard to a quality like height, intelligence, or speed, and is therefore readily identifiable.

*This isn't the best camping country.*
*...the easiest way of finding water.*
*Birmingham is one of the largest cities in Europe.*
*That's the nicest thing anybody has ever said to me.*

## Specific uses of the definite article

Here are some examples where the superlative is formed with 'most' instead of '-est'.

*The most difficult moments came at night.*
*But the most powerful censor remains the audience.*

Superlatives are often used on their own, without a noun following.

*The old jokes are the best.*
*There are some forty different species in the kangaroo family. The largest is the red kangaroo.*

**The** is sometimes left out after a link verb such as 'be'.

*Which work pattern is easiest?*
*It's the butter fat that is hardest to digest.*

However, it is not possible to leave out **the** when the superlative is followed by a phrase or clause specifying the group or place involved.

*The number of teachers per child is the highest in the world.*
*Into the envelope - which had to be the largest I could find - I also tucked used guide books and useful addresses.*

Here the definite article must be kept; you cannot say 'The number of teachers per child is highest in the world'.

There are other cases where the meaning would be different if the definite article was left out.

*Beef is nicest slightly underdone.*

Here we are comparing the different ways of doing beef; if you say 'Beef is the nicest', you are comparing different meats.

**Note 1** It is possible to use the indefinite article before 'best', but only when 'best' and the noun after it together form a fixed expression, such as 'best friend' or 'best seller'.

*Is that what a best friend is for?*
*You ought to write a novel about it, could be a best seller.*

**Note 2** 'Most' has other meanings: as a determiner, meaning 'the majority of', and as an adverb, where it is very similar to 'very'.

*...the sweat glands that the platypus, like most mammals, has in its skin.*
*We have a most important matter to discuss.*

▶ Exercise 11

## 4.12 Unique adjectives

There are some other adjectives which, like superlative adjectives, are used to identify unique things, and so the definite article is used before them.

*They even use the same lawyers.*
*The next attack took place four hours later.*
*He was the only doctor I knew.*
*I began the last section of the book.*
*Pour the right amount into each bottle.*

Here is a list of adjectives which are used in this way:

| | | | |
|---|---|---|---|
| first | next | principal | ultimate |
| following | only | right | usual |
| last | opposite | same | wrong |
| main | present | sole | |

This is not a rule, only a strong tendency; the indefinite article sometimes occurs with them (except with 'next', 'following', and 'same').

*He paid a last visit to America.*
*The answer is not to ignore a first child.*

The indefinite article can be used before 'only' when it is used in the expressions 'only child', 'only son', and 'only daughter'.

*I was an only child.*

**Note 1** The definite article is often used with 'wrong' even when it does not make sense to talk about only one wrong possibility.

*If he gives the wrong answer the machine stops.*
*We are all in the wrong business.*

In these cases there is possibly more than one wrong answer or business. However, there are some cases where the indefinite article is used.

*We've taken a wrong turn.*

**Note 2** 'Same' often appears without a following noun; 'first' and 'last' often occur followed by an 'of'-phrase, rather than a noun.

*The same is true for men.*
*It was the first of many adjustments we had to make in our life-style.*
*The last of the official engagements was the pre-tour dinner.*

**Note 3** 'Next' and 'last' are commonly used in time expressions without **the** (for example, 'next week').

**Note 4** The ordinal numbers 'second', 'third', and so on occur with the indefinite article more often than 'first'.

*Now, it seemed, there might be a third choice.*

▶ Exercise 12

## 4.13 Using the definite article at the beginning of stories

Consider this sentence, which is the first line of 'The Catbird Seat' by James Thurber.

*Mr Martin bought the pack of Camels on Monday night.*

Why 'the pack'? It would be perfectly normal to say 'a pack of Camels' (a brand of cigarette), especially as the reader has not been told anything about it before. The answer is that the writer is indicating in this way that the reader will shortly be told more about the pack. Here is another example, from the beginning of 'The Lord of the Flies' by William Golding:

*The boy with fair hair lowered himself down the last few feet of rock and began to pick his way towards the lagoon.*

The boy and the lagoon have not previously been mentioned. It is only later that the reader learns more about the boy, where he is, and why he is there.

This is a stylistic device which you probably will not need to use, but you will need to understand it. Titles of stories and novels are similar: 'The Catbird Seat', 'The Man Who Knew How', 'The Letter', 'The Enemy', and so on.

## 4.14 Stressed 'the' meaning 'best'

People sometimes stress the definite article to indicate that something is the best, most fashionable, or only thing of a particular kind. For example, someone might say 'It's *the* place to go' (with **the** pronounced /ði:/) when referring to a discotheque or club which is very good or fashionable.

*Billiards is the game.*
*The foregoing scenario in no way pretends to present the answer to urban transportation problems.*

See also section 7.13 for another situation when **the** is stressed.

# 5 Articles with generic reference

## 5.1 Introduction: different types of generic reference

At the start of Chapter 4 we made a distinction between two types of reference: **specific reference** and **generic reference**. Here we are going to look at generic reference, that is, when we use a noun to refer to a whole group or class of something, to generalize about all the possible members of a group.

There are five patterns which you can use to refer generically. These are:

1) no article + plural count noun

*It's astonishing what _dogs_ can know.*

2) no article + uncount noun

*_Passion_, whether it's love or hatred, can involve a lot of suffering.*

3) the indefinite article + singular count noun

*_A dog_ likes to eat far more than _a human being_.*

This pattern is discussed in section 5.2.

4) the definite article + singular count noun

*_The gorilla_ is a shy retiring creature.*

This pattern is discussed in section 5.3.

5) the definite article + plural nationality noun, or adjective

*_The Chinese_, in their turn, became the bitter enemies of the Russians. It is our treatment of _the old_ which most shocks students of our culture.*

This pattern is discussed in sections 5.4 and 5.5.

WARNING  Some books give the impression that these different patterns have exactly the same meaning, that you can use one instead of another, as in these sentences: 'Lions/A lion/The lion can be dangerous'. This is not always true, however; they can have different meanings, and patterns 3, 4 and 5 are all limited in some way, especially 5; you cannot use the definite article with all nouns in the plural to refer generically; if you say 'The lions are dangerous' it does not have a generic meaning.

Of these patterns, the commonest are 1 and 2; you can use them in most situations.

*_Coffee_ and _tea_ are not good drinks for _children_.*

Pattern 1 can often be used instead of 3 and 4; you could also say 'Dogs like to eat far more than human beings' and 'Gorillas are shy, retiring creatures'.

▶ Exercise 5

## 5.2 Singular count nouns with the indefinite article

You can use a singular count noun with the indefinite article to refer to something as a representative of its class.

*An actor must learn to live with criticism.*
*An adult porpoise is six feet long.*
*It is always fatal to ask an expert.*

You cannot use this pattern when you want to talk about the location or existence of a type of animal, thing, or person; for example, you cannot say 'A ring-tailed lemur lives in Madagascar'; you would have to say 'Ring-tailed lemurs live in Madagascar' or 'The ring-tailed lemur lives in Madagascar'.

This use is common in explanations of meanings and in some dictionary definitions.

*In grammar, a noun is a word which is used to refer to a person, a thing, or an abstract idea.*
*A mountain is bigger and higher than a hill.*

As mentioned above in section 5.1, you can also use the plural without an article to express the same meaning: 'Mountains are bigger and higher than hills'.

Note 'Any' sometimes has a similar but more emphatic meaning.

*The greatest threat to any actor is the presumption that knowledge can be automatically transposed into experience.*

▶ Exercises 1, 2, and 5

## 5.3 Singular count nouns with the definite article

You can use the definite article with some singular count nouns to make a generalization.

*The primary responsibility lies with the employer.*

Here you are using one employer as the typical example of the class. This way of referring to a type of person or thing is used mainly when writers or speakers are generalizing on a topic of professional relevance to them, usually in a formal context.

This pattern is common when talking about regular participants or roles in a situation. For example, someone talking or writing about education might want to refer in general to 'the teacher', 'the learner' or 'the classroom'. Here are some examples of topics.

| TOPIC | ROLES |
|-------|-------|
| education | the teacher, the learner/pupil, the classroom |
| health care | the doctor, the nurse, the patient |
| industrial relations | the employer, the employee, the shop-steward |
| the communication process | the speaker, the listener, the writer, the reader |

*The third task of the teacher is criticism.*
*In very general terms then the role of the shop-steward can be broken down into three main parts.*

This pattern is often used when talking about species of animals and birds.

*The red squirrel is steadily dying out.*

It is also commonly used when doctors or other people are generalizing professionally about parts of the body.

*This may flatten that side of the head. It won't hurt the brain.*
*This chapter deals with the lower part of the leg.*

(See section 6.13 for another way in which the definite article is used with parts of the body.)

Inventions and technological developments are often talked about in this way.

*...as a previous generation was taught to speak into the telephone.*
*The computer has a flexibility of function which is unique.*

You can also generalize about rooms in this way.

*The kitchen can be a very suitable place to practise exercise.*

▶ Exercises 3, 4, and 5


## 5.4 Nationality words with the definite article

You can use the definite article when referring generically to nations or racial groups.

*And he helped the French and the Russians do the same.*

# Articles with generic reference

With some groups, you use **the** and the nationality adjective. You do this when the adjective ends in '-sh', '-ch', '-ese', or '-ss' (unless there is a different word which is used to refer to a person belonging to that group, for example 'Swede' or 'Turk', which does not end in '-man').

*...roast beef, Yorkshire pudding and 'two veg', at one time the regular Sunday dinner of the British.*
*The Dutch are planning to do that by 1994.*
*The Chinese have their own version of this proverb.*
*The Swiss see no need to change their policy of 'armed neutrality'.*

With other groups, you can use **the** and the plural form of the noun used to refer to a person belonging to that group.

*As fighters, the Canadians, Australians and New Zealanders had an especially high reputation.*
*What the Africans made of him will never be known.*
*The Poles had struggled for freedom in a series of wars and revolutions.*

(When referring to the people of Spain, you can say either 'the Spanish' or 'the Spaniards'.)

Of course, the plural without **the** can be used generically too, as any plural can (see section 5.1).

*I like Americans. Americans have consciences.*

The use of **the**, as in the example below, stresses that you are referring to the nation as a group, especially a political group.

*It is difficult to see how the Americans could keep up the fight.*

**Note 1** The definite article with a plural nationality noun does not always show generic reference; it could also be a case of specific reference (see section 4.1).

*Between her and the Americans was a table load of Japanese.*

**Note 2** These words always begin with a capital letter; and they are followed by the plural form of a verb even if they do not look plural.

*...because the French were less devout.*
*It seems to me that the British are too often their own worst critics.*

▶ Exercise 6

## 5.5 Adjectives with the definite article

A combination of the definite article and an adjective (without a noun) can be used to refer to all the people with that characteristic. 'The poor' means 'people who are poor'.

*...the exploitation of the poor by the rich, of the weak by the powerful.*
*It seems that the unemployed can be kept out of sight.*
*...though the dead are believed to be alive in some sense.*
*Youth is wasted on the young.*

Many adjectives can be used in this way; here are some common ones.

| | | | | |
|---|---|---|---|---|
| aged | educated | injured | powerful | unemployed |
| blind | elderly | living | rich | weak |
| brave | free | needy | sick | wealthy |
| dead | handicapped | old | starving | wounded |
| deaf | homeless | oppressed | strong | young |
| disabled | hungry | poor | uneducated | |

They behave like nouns in the plural and are followed by a plural verb.

*The rich have not responded.*

For other combinations between the definite article and adjectives on their own, see sections 4.11, 4.12, 8.9, and 8.10.

▶ Exercise 7

## 5.6 'Man'

A special case of pattern 2 is 'man', usually meaning all human beings rather than all male human beings.

*...if man does not face reality.*
*...while modern man was evolving.*

There are many other ways of referring generically to human beings: 'people,' 'mankind', 'the human race', or simply 'we'.

*People like stability.*
*We all need vitamins in our food.*

'The man' is never used for generic reference. 'A man' is sometimes used, but this often sounds old-fashioned.

# 6 Article use with certain groups of words

## 6.1 Introduction

In this chapter we will look at how articles are used with certain groups of words; article usage with these words can be a problem for learners. Sometimes this is because the words have different meanings which can be reflected in the choice of article; for example, the difference between 'a bus', which means a particular vehicle which runs on roads, and 'the bus', which can have this meaning but which can also refer to a particular form of transport, for example:

*The bus left every half hour*.

This does not mean that there was only one bus (vehicle) which repeated its departure every 30 minutes; we are talking about a bus service involving several buses. Systems, services, or institutions can be referred to in this way. These are dealt with in detail in sections 6.2, 6.3, 6.4, and 6.5.

In other sections you will find information on groups of words where the use of articles seems to be unpredictable but in fact is not; the presence of different articles with the same word can be explained by the rules given elsewhere in this book. These groups of words are included as a reference for learners.

## 6.2 Media and communications

You can refer to systems of mass communication and the media by using a noun with the definite article (or sometimes by using a noun without an article). In this way you can distinguish them from actual objects; 'a radio' will always be a particular object, but 'the radio' could refer to a system, as in this example.

*We gather facts and attitudes from the press, the television and the radio.*

Words in this category are:

| | | | | |
|---|---|---|---|---|
| (the) television | the box | the telephone | the press | the post (Br) |
| (the) telly | (the) radio | the phone | the papers | the mail (Am) |
| (the) TV | the news | the newspapers | the paper | |

When referring to television as a form of entertainment or communication, you can use the definite article (which tends to be informal) or no article.

*They go on the television and smoke drugs in front of the viewers.*

*He isn't as serious as he is on television.*

The abbreviations, 'TV' and 'telly' can be used in the same way, although 'TV' tends to occur without an article in this sense. 'Telly' is an informal alternative; another informal expression is 'the box' (always with **the**).

*I don't want to be seen on the telly.*
*...anyone whose face appears regularly in newspapers and on TV.*
*...a constant background of telly or radio.*

If someone says 'on the television' it can mean two things: 'physically on' ("There's a photo of him on the television"), or 'being broadcast' ("There's a good programme on the television tonight"). If you say 'on television', only the second meaning is possible. (See section 6.4 for more information on 'television'.)

You can refer to radio as a means of communication with either the definite article or no article.

*I just heard her speaking on the radio.*
*He had already become a climbing spokesman on radio.*

When using 'telephone' or 'phone' to refer to a means of communication, you use the definite article.

*A large part of Linda's day is spent on the telephone.*
*Haig and Nixon are regularly on the phone with each other.*

Here we are not thinking of one particular telephone; we are more interested in the form of communication.

There are also the expressions 'by telephone' and 'by phone' in which 'telephone' and 'phone' refer to the the system of communication, although there is no article.

*...an attempt to reach her at the camp by telephone.*

You speak of 'the newspapers' or 'the papers' when referring to newspapers as a form of media. The meaning is similar to 'the press'.

*The papers are saying how unusual it is.*
*How would it look in the papers?*

Sometimes 'the paper' is also used to mean newspapers generally, not one particular newspaper.

*This is what we read in the paper.*

When you use 'post' (American equivalent 'mail') to refer to a system of communication, you use the definite article.

*One morning there arrived through the post an amazing letter.*

# Article use with certain groups of words

However, there is also the expression 'by post' which refers to the service.

*He acquired the necessary reference books by post.*

▶ Exercise 1


## 6.3 Means of transport

You can use the definite article with words like 'train' or 'bus' when you are referring to a whole transport system, rather than to an individual train or bus.

*She sent a cable to her husband and caught the plane back to New York.*
*How long does it take on the train?*

In these examples, the speaker does not mean one particular plane or train; there may be several possibilities. The speaker is naming the form or system of transport. Here is a list of words in this category.

| | | | |
|---|---|---|---|
| boat | hovercraft | train | underground (Br) |
| bus | plane | tram | |
| ferry | subway (Am) | tube (Br) | |

Here are some more examples.

*Then I saw him get into a cab, although the subway was good enough as a rule.*
*I walked to the tube instead of spending money on a taxi.*

'Boat' and 'ferry' are used in this way but not 'ship'.

*...the vast new Lenin Bridge over the Volga which had replaced the ferry.*

'Taxi', 'car' and 'bicycle' are not used in this way, because they do not offer a systematic means of transport; if you say to someone 'Take the car', you must be referring to a particular car.

With 'underground', 'tube', and 'subway', you can use the definite article to refer not only to the form of transport, but also to the location.

*I am alone in the underground waiting for a train.*

All these words can be used after 'by' without an article to describe the form of transport used, for example: 'by bus', 'by train', 'by plane'.

*I don't often travel by bus.*
*He got himself back to London the quickest way, by train and plane.*

You can also use the following words after 'by' without an article.

| | | | |
|---|---|---|---|
| air | cab | road | taxi |
| bicycle | car | sea | |
| bike | rail | ship | |

▶ Exercise 2

## 6.4 Forms of entertainment

When you are talking about someone going to enjoy a form of entertainment you use the definite article with the word for the form of entertainment. Words like this are: 'cinema' (Am 'movies'), 'theatre', 'opera', 'ballet'.

*Let's go to the movies.*
*You have seen things. You have been to the opera, the ballet, the theatre.*

Here we are not thinking of a particular performance of an opera or ballet, or a particular theatre building, but just of the form of entertainment.

'Cinema', 'theatre', 'opera', and 'ballet', as well as 'dance', 'film', and 'television', can be used as uncount nouns without an article to refer to the art form.

*...supreme artists of dance and theatre.*
*...a very fine piece of cinema.*
*Television can be an art medium.*

▶ Exercise 3

## 6.5 Institutions in society

There are certain establishments of human society which are referred to without an article when we think of them as institutions in general rather than as specific buildings or individual places.

*He was finally admitted to hospital with an ulcerated leg.*
*...after our first victory in court.*

Here is a list of words that can be used like this.

| | | | |
|---|---|---|---|
| church | court | jail | school |
| college | hospital | prison | university |

Normally, when you are using these words to talk about buildings they are count nouns and article usage with them is straightforward. But when you want to suggest that they are being

43

used for their intended purpose there is no article; that is, worshipping in church, studying in school/college/university, receiving medical care in hospital, being a prisoner in prison or jail, legal action in court. Often there is a different way of expressing the idea: 'She's at university' is similar to saying 'She's a student'.

Here are some more examples.

*...once he is taken home from <u>hospital</u>.*
*In the morning all the peasants went to <u>church</u>.*
*He left <u>school</u> at seventeen.*
*...to decide whether to go to <u>court</u> or not.*
*His parents couldn't afford to send him to <u>university</u>.*
*After 11 days in <u>prison</u> they were released.*

There are some differences between British and American usage here. Firstly, Americans say 'the hospital' instead of 'hospital' for institutional reference. Secondly, the word 'university' is not used in this way; the American equivalent of 'at university' is 'in college'.

'Bed' behaves in a similar way; without an article it means the place where we sleep or rest, not a particular object.

*She went to <u>bed</u> and slept lightly.*

▶ Exercise 4

## 6.6 Shops and other businesses

Shops and other businesses that are regular features in towns or cities can be used with the definite article when you do not want to pick out a particular one.

*He might have been to <u>the barber's</u> to please his mother.*
*He's at <u>the dentist's</u>.*
*It enables you to put money into <u>the bank</u> and withdraw it.*
*Mother sent me to <u>the butcher's</u> to get a nice joint of beef.*

Some words like this are:

| | | |
|---|---|---|
| baker's | dentist's | hairdresser's |
| bank | doctor's | post office |
| barber's | greengrocer's | pub |

In these cases the activity is as important as the place. You go 'to the post office' to get some stamps, 'to the bank' to get some money, 'to the barber's/hairdresser's' to have your hair cut, 'to the dentist's' to have your teeth filled, and so on.

If you want to have a drink you can say 'Let's go to the pub' without having a particular one in mind. But of course the difference is not always clear, or important.

*When he tired of painting he went to <u>the pub</u>.*

This could mean one particular pub that we know about, or any pub; the important thing is that he needed a drink or some company.

▶ Exercise 5


## 6.7 Musical instruments

When you are talking about someone's ability to play a musical instrument you use the definite article.

*She already played <u>the guitar</u>.*
*I became interested in <u>the piano</u> again.*

This does not mean one particular guitar or piano, as an object; we are talking about the ability. So the second example above means '...interested in playing the piano...'.

If you want to talk about roles in a musical group or in a piece of music you use no article.

*...making up an unusual trio of <u>trumpet</u>, <u>guitar</u>, and <u>drums</u>.*
*I don't think I know of any duets for <u>piano</u> and <u>trumpet</u>.*

There is also no article after 'on', meaning 'playing'.

*...a recording featuring Harris's old pal Ray Brown on <u>bass</u>.*

▶ Exercise 6


## 6.8 Geographical oppositions

You use the definite article before a number of nouns which indicate geographical alternatives, for example 'the town' - 'the country' and 'the sea' - 'the land'.

*There are compensations in <u>the town</u>, particularly for older children.*
*I'd gone to <u>the country</u> with some friends.*
*...tourists who take their holidays in <u>the mountains</u> rather than at the seaside.*
*...rain hammering <u>the land</u> and <u>the forest</u>.*

We are not referring to a particular place, for example a particular town or forest. We are talking about the types of landscape or geographical environments where people live, work, or go for holidays.

Here are some words you can use like this.

| the city | the desert | the land | the sea |
|---|---|---|---|
| the country | the forest | the mountains | the seaside |
| the countryside | the jungle | the plains | the town |

'The country' in this context means areas where there are no towns or cities. You can sometimes use 'the countryside' with a similar meaning.

'Sea' is used in certain prepositional expressions without **the**.

...*after he'd gone to <u>sea</u>.*
...*the main danger to naval forces and shipping at <u>sea</u>.*

▶ Exercise 7

## 6.9 Directions

Nouns indicating directions, such as 'north', 'south', 'east', and 'west', and 'left' and 'right', have the definite article.

*Then circle to <u>the left</u>.*
...*across the border to <u>the south</u>.*
...*just to <u>the north</u> of the little bay.*

'North', 'south', 'east', and 'west' can also be used with the definite article to refer to one part of a country; if they refer to an accepted region they sometimes begin with a capital letter (see section 7.2).

...*while she was away in <u>the north</u>.*
...*in <u>the North</u> of England.*

You can use 'the left' and 'the right' to describe the political movements which support socialism and capitalism respectively; 'left' and 'right' may start with a capital letter in this case.

...*the parties of <u>the left</u>.*
...*pressure by <u>the Left</u>.*

**Note** These words are also used as adverbs without an article.

*I was again heading <u>north</u>.*

▶ Exercise 8

## 6.10 Periods of time

Article use with the names of periods of time is best explained according to the different types of period; this is done below. See also section 7.8 for names of religious festivals and other special days.

## Seasons

When you are talking about a specific occurrence of a season, you usually use the definite article.

*You'll feel better in the spring.*

In dates you say, for example, 'spring 1974' but 'the spring of 1974'.

When you are talking generally about a season or what happens in a season, you can use the definite article or no article.

*I do some rock-climbing in the summer, ski in the winter.*
*It was a wide, high-ceilinged room, excessively cold in winter.*

Note that you do not usually use the definite article after 'It is' or 'It was'.

*Now it was truly spring.*

You can pick out one particular period using the indefinite article.

*I spent a summer in the Cyclades.*

In American English it is more common to refer to the seasons with the definite article (except after 'next' and 'last').

## Months and days of the week

With the names of months and days of the week you usually use no article when you want to relate a period to the present, for example 'on Tuesday', 'in May'.

*...at their meeting in Luxembourg on Tuesday.*
*...since it first appeared in December.*

However, you can use the indefinite article with the days of the week to identify one day of the week in general.

*Don't do it on a Monday.*
*It was always washing on a Monday and baking on a Wednesday.*

Compare this with 'He bought it on Monday', meaning 'last Monday'.

You can use the definite or indefinite article with qualification or modification to refer to one particular day.

*...Monday April 17, an ordinary Monday.*
*...not later than the second Monday in May.*

A definite article without modification suggests a day in the week you are talking about.

*It got under way at two o'clock on the Tuesday, having been meant to start on the previous Friday.*

47

# Article use with certain groups of words

## Parts of the day

You can use articles in the normal way when referring to a part of one particular day. You can also use the definite article when you want to stress one part as opposed to others.

*The best times to take the temperature are in the first part of the morning and late in the afternoon.*
*Traditionally cooking was carried out in the evening.*
*Sometimes I wake in the night in a panic.*
*...if you swim only during the day.*

Here 'day' does not refer to a 24-hour period, but only to part of one (as opposed to night); if you want to make this clear you can use 'daytime'.

*...especially in the daytime.*

'Night' is used after 'at' and 'by' without an article. You can also say 'by day'.

*The practice of giving a baby a bottle of water at night is a bad one.*

## Longer periods

Words like 'day', 'week', 'month', 'year', and so on, are typically count nouns and so can be used with both the definite and indefinite articles.

*...the day after the trial.*
*She had loved him for over a year.*
*A week later she woke up screaming.*

Like 'day', 'week' has two meanings. It can be used to refer to a period of seven days, as above, or to the days between two weekends. The expression 'during the week' can be used to mean 'on the days between weekends'.

*People used to come at the weekends, but during the week I was alone in that huge house.*

## Specific periods

Names of decades, centuries and historic periods, which refer to only one particular period, have the definite article, for example 'the nineteen-eighties', 'the nineteenth century', 'the iron age'. They are an example of unique reference (see section 4.8).

*...the sexual revolution of the sixties.*

## 'Past', 'present', and 'future'

'Past', 'present', and 'future' generally have the definite article.

*...the dangers in thinking only of the present.*

*...plans for <u>the future</u>.*
*...more people than I had ever been responsible for in <u>the past.</u>*

But 'present' and 'future' can be used after 'at' and 'in' respectively
with no article.

*...since there is no certain answer <u>at present</u>.*
*Try to remember it <u>in future</u>.*

In American English 'in the future' is used rather than 'in future'.

It is possible to use an indefinite article when talking about the life
of one particular person: 'He has a future', 'a man with a past'.

▶ Exercise 9

## 6.11 Illnesses

Article usage with the names of illnesses and other conditions is
sometimes inconsistent, and can vary with the same word.
Normally nouns referring to illnesses are uncount and do not have
an indefinite or definite article.

*...evidence that they caused <u>cancer</u>.*

Here is a list of common words like this.

| | | | |
|---|---|---|---|
| AIDS | diarrhoea | malaria | tuberculosis |
| anaemia | hepatitis | pneumonia | typhoid |
| appendicitis | herpes | rabies | yellow fever |
| cancer | influenza | rheumatism | |
| cholera | laryngitis | smallpox | |
| diabetes | leukaemia | tonsillitis | |

'Cancer' can also be count, but combinations with it are uncount,
for example 'lung cancer'.

With the names of some common infectious diseases the definite
article can be used, as well as no article, but it is not as common.
This applies to 'flu' (but not 'influenza'), 'measles', 'mumps', and
'chickenpox'.

*She's coming down with <u>the flu</u>.*
*I had a mild attack of <u>flu</u>.*
*...unlike <u>the measles</u> itself.*
*...the first symptoms of <u>measles</u>.*

The names of less specific conditions, such as 'cold', 'chill', or
'cough', are treated as simple count nouns.

*...when someone has <u>a cold</u>.*

Words ending in '-ache' behave in different ways, in British
English. 'Earache', 'toothache', 'backache', 'stomach-ache', and so

49

on can be uncount or count, so you can say 'I've got earache' and
'I've got an earache'.

*He was suffering from severe earache.*
*One morning she developed an earache.*
*...various infusions which she used for sore eyes, toothache and*
*muscular pains.*
*...when a woman with a toothache was brought to us.*

'Headache', however, is a count noun, and so you can have 'a
headache' or regular 'headaches', but you cannot say 'I've got
headache'.

*Next morning she complained of a headache.*

In American English, all '-ache' words are count nouns, so it is not
possible to say 'I've got earache', and so on.

▶ Exercise 10

## 6.12 Meals

You can refer to meals without using an article when you are
talking in general about the standard meals of the day.

*Tim had dinner in the hotel.*
*Breakfast was already waiting for her.*

If you are talking about individual meals, you can use the nouns
'breakfast', 'lunch', and so on as count nouns with an appropriate
article. When used like this, the nouns are usually qualified or
modified (see sections 4.9 and 3.7); you do not normally say 'I had a
breakfast.'

*...the main virtue of a hot breakfast.*
*...after a relaxed breakfast.*

'Lunch' and 'dinner' can also be used alone with the indefinite
article to mean a special formal occasion.

*Afterwards, Her Royal Highness attended a dinner at the Castle*
*Hotel.*

It would be unusual to say 'I've been invited to a breakfast' since
breakfast is not usually a formal occasion.

## 6.13 Parts of the body

Names of parts of the body, like 'hand', 'face', and 'knee', are
usually count nouns used with the indefinite or definite article
according to the standard rules of use (see Chapters 3 and 4). We

have also seen a special use of the definite article to refer generically to body parts (section 5.3).

There is also a use where we are thinking of parts of the body not as separate organs or limbs but as locations on the body. For this you can use the definite article.

*They might dash out later and stab them in the back.*
*She had the urge to beat him over the head.*

It is possible to use the definite article with a singular noun even when there are two possible parts.

*Stein took Breslow by the arm.*
*...to shake him by the hand.*
*It bit her on the leg.*
*He was wounded in the leg too.*

Here there is no suggestion that Breslow has only one arm (mentioned before) or that 'he' has only one leg; the part of the body is all that is important, not which side.

You use the definite article like this when the noun referring to the body part is included in a prepositional phrase ('in the back', 'by the arm') after a verb of touching or injuring ('shake', 'bite'), and the person whose body you are referring to has just been mentioned ('them', 'Breslow').

When the noun comes straight after a verb such as 'grab' or after a verb and a preposition, for example 'step on', you have to use a possessive determiner like 'their' or 'his'; for example, you have to say 'I stepped on his foot' not 'I stepped on the foot'. Sometimes there are alternatives: 'I shook him by the hand' or 'I shook his hand'.

*The black-haired youth grabbed her arm and shook her.*
*Robert touched her cheek.*

You can also use the definite article when referring to a touch, blow, or pain.

*...giving me a friendly pat on the shoulder.*
*I have a pain in the side.*

▶ Exercise 11

## 6.14 Special roles

Some nouns can refer to a special, unique role held by a person in a particular situation (for example, a government or business). When they are used like this, you can leave out the definite article.

*...when he was <u>President</u>.*
*It was nearly 40 years before she became <u>Queen</u>.*
*...Mr John Hume, <u>leader</u> of the Social and Democratic Labour Party.*

It would be unnatural to leave in the definite article and say 'when he was the President' or 'she became the Queen', although you can leave it in when the noun is followed by 'of'. Some words commonly used in this way are:

| | | | |
|---|---|---|---|
| author | chairman | king | queen |
| best man | chairperson | leader | secretary |
| boss | director | manager | treasurer |
| captain | goalkeeper | president | |
| centre forward | head | prime minister | |

The context is very important. In a gang, one person can be 'leader'; in a football team, one person can be 'captain', 'centre forward', or 'goalkeeper'; at a wedding one person can be 'best man'; in a country one person can be 'king', 'queen', 'president', or 'prime minister'. Many other nouns can be used in this way in a particular context.

Note that when you are talking about a person rather than describing someone's role you need an article.

*The President had issued a sympathetic reply.*
*The Queen then abandoned the project.*

▶ Exercise 12

## 6.15 Grammatical terms

The words that linguists use to describe certain words or constructions in English often have the definite article. We talk about 'the past participle', 'the present tense', 'the active voice', or nouns which are 'in the singular'.

*In clauses like these you use a verb which is in <u>the present tense</u>.*
*With most verbs which end in 'e' <u>the present participle</u> is formed by substituting 'ing' for the final 'e'.*

With these terms you can use the indefinite article if you want to describe one particular instance: 'Singing is a present participle'. You could also say 'Singing is an example of the present participle' or 'Singing is the present participle of sing'.

The most important cases in this book are of course 'the definite article' and 'the indefinite article'. Here are some examples taken from earlier chapters.

*The indefinite article has two forms, both in speech and writing.*
*However, it is not true to say that all these nouns only occur with the*
*definite article.*

You can use the indefinite article if you want to pick out one
particular instance, as in 'He used an indefinite article where I
would have used a definite article'.

▶ Exercise 13

# 7 Articles and proper nouns

## 7.1 Introduction: proper nouns

The other chapters have all looked at article usage with **common nouns**, nouns which can be applied to items of the same kind: this black animal is 'a cat', those creatures in the pet shop window are 'cats', the piece of meat that is missing was eaten by 'the cat', and so on. 'Cat' is a common noun. But when we refer to a particular cat by using its name, for example 'Blackie', then this is a **proper noun**.

Proper nouns represent the names of many things: people, animals, countries, cities, buildings, streets, rivers, mountains, newspapers, and so on.

*...the house that overlooked the Thames at Marlow.*
*...in the collection of Queen Elizabeth II at Buckingham Palace.*
*...Charles Clarke's book on Everest, with its fine photographs.*

You can recognize proper nouns in a number of ways:

● in writing they start with a capital letter: 'England'. (Not all nouns that start with a capital are proper nouns, for example, nationality nouns like 'the Italians'.)

● if they are made up of more than one word they cannot be split up: it is not possible to say 'Hyde beautiful Park'; you must say 'beautiful Hyde Park'.

● like uncount nouns (see Chapter 2) you cannot normally use them with the indefinite article or use them in the plural (but see section 7.14).

● like unique nouns (see section 4.8) they typically refer to only one thing (or group of things); 'the Orkneys' refers to a particular group of islands off the north coast of Scotland, whereas the common noun 'islands' can refer to any group of islands.

With proper nouns the use of articles is fixed; some have the definite article and some have no article, and except in unusual cases there is no change.

*...the determination of the governments in Dublin and London.*
*The changes in the Times were gradual.*

There are a number of guidelines as to which proper nouns have the definite article and which have no article, and the rest of this chapter tries to show you these. But it cannot account for all cases, so when you encounter a proper noun you should pay attention to whether it has a definite article or not.

There are also some general hints:

● plural proper nouns have the definite article: 'the Azores', 'the West Indies'.

● constructions made up of two nouns separated by 'of' tend to have **the**: 'the House of Commons'.

## 7.2 Geographical and place names with the definite article

You use the definite article with the following types of geographical or place names:

**Groups of islands**, for example: the British Isles, the Hawaiian Islands.

*...a deposit account in <u>the Channel Islands</u>.*
*It was his custom to spend his holidays in <u>the Scilly Isles</u>.*

Sometimes there are alternatives; for example, you can say 'the Orkney Islands' or 'the Orkneys'.

**Mountain ranges and groups of hills**, for example: the Alps, the Himalayas, the North Downs.

*I had never climbed in <u>the Alps</u> in winter.*

Sometimes there are alternatives; for example, you can say 'the Rocky Mountains' or 'the Rockies'.

**Geographical regions**, for example: the Midlands, the Middle East, the Punjab, the Crimea, the Dordogne, the South of England.

*The home-ownership rate in <u>the South East of England</u> is higher than in <u>the North</u>.*
*...in a mill in <u>the Dordogne</u>.*

Note that these are different from political and administrative regions (see section 7.3).

**Deserts**, for example: the Sahara, the Gobi Desert.

*...Africa south of <u>the Sahara</u>.*

**Rivers, streams and canals**, for example: the Thames, the Mississippi, the Nile, the Panama Canal. With rivers you can include 'river' as part of the name: the River Severn.

*...along the flood plains of rivers like <u>the Soar</u> and <u>the Severn</u>.*
*<u>The Suez Canal</u> was blocked.*
*...the annual conferences held at Konigswinter on <u>the River Rhine</u>.*

**Seas and oceans**, for example: the Indian Ocean, the North Sea.

*Here the Baltic Sea narrows to the Kattegat.*
*Bicycling across America. From the Atlantic to the Pacific.*

Sometimes there are alternatives with or without 'sea' or 'ocean'; for example, you can say 'the Atlantic' or 'the Atlantic Ocean', 'the Mediterranean' or 'the Mediterranean Sea'.

**Other sea features.** Other features of seas and coastlines usually have the definite article, for example: the English Channel, the Straits of Dover, the Gulf of Mexico (for bays see below).

*...an attempt to cross the English Channel in a small plane.*
*...on the north shore of the Firth of Forth.*
*...a blockade of the Straits of Hormuz.*

WARNING   On maps the definite article is usually not shown.

▶ Exercises 1 and 2

## 7.3 Geographical and place names without an article

With the following types of proper nouns there is usually no article:

**Continents**, such as: Europe, America, Africa, Asia, Antarctica.

*As a result Africa was full of refugees.*

But you say 'the African Continent'.

**Countries**, such as: Britain, France, Germany, China, India, Australia.

*...some of the allies, notably France and Canada.*

However, some names of countries have the definite article, in particular those which contain common nouns: the Union of Soviet Socialist Republics, the United States of America, the United Kingdom. This is the same with abbreviated alternatives: the USSR, the USA, the UK, and so on.

*...the 1920s car sales boom in the USA.*

Sometimes a name without **the** has an official alternative with **the**: China or the People's Republic of China.

Plurals also have **the**: the Netherlands, the Philippines. With the names of countries that have developed from geographical regions there are often two possibilities, with or without the definite article: Sudan or the Sudan, Yemen or the Yemen, Argentina or the Argentine, Cameroun or the Cameroons, Ukraine or the Ukraine, Ivory Coast or the Ivory Coast. The tendency is to use the form without the definite article.

*...African leaders meeting in <u>Ivory Coast</u>.*

**Political and administrative regions of countries**, for example: California, Hampshire.

*...in a little valley of <u>Bavaria.</u>*
*...at his home in <u>Kent.</u>*

**Villages, towns and cities**, for example: Chiddingstone, Tonbridge, London.

*A car passed them, heading towards <u>London</u>.*

There is the exceptional case of 'The Hague', where the definite article is a fixed part of the place name.

**Bays**.

*He worked as a tugboat man on <u>San Francisco Bay</u>.*
*...a mystery tour round <u>Morecambe Bay</u>.*

However, where there are two nouns separated by 'of', the definite article is used, for example: the Bay of Bengal, the Bay of Biscay, the Bay of Pigs, the Bay of Fundy.

*...the resort of Biarritz, on <u>the Bay of Biscay</u>.*

**Lakes**.

*...overlooking the calm waters of <u>Lake Michigan.</u>*

There are some exceptions: the Great Salt Lake, the Lake of Geneva (also Lake Geneva).

**Individual islands**, for example: Ireland, Bermuda, Sicily, Borneo.

*...their breeding grounds south-west of <u>Bermuda</u>.*
*...the statues of <u>Easter Island</u>.*

However, there are exceptions when two nouns have 'of' in between: the Isle of Man, the Isle of Wight.

**Individual mountains**, for example: Ben Nevis, (Mount) Everest, Mont Blanc, Mount Fuji, and so on.

*They simply wanted to go and climb <u>Everest</u>.*

Some names of foreign mountains keep the definite article: the Matterhorn.

▶ Exercises 1 and 2

## 7.4 Names of buildings and institutions

There is no obvious rule for names of buildings and institutions; they are dealt with group by group in the following pages.

## Articles and proper nouns

The following names typically have the definite article (although on maps the definite article is usually not shown):

**Hotels, restaurants and pubs**, for example: the Ritz, the Hilton, the Copper Kettle, the Royal Oak.

*I haven't the least idea how many rooms there are in <u>the Ritz</u>.*

But restaurants whose name is the possessive form of a person's name have no definite article: Luigi's.

**Theatres and cinemas**, for example: the Odeon, the Globe.

*Everything would now depend on the first night at <u>the Lyric</u>.*

Note that the definite article may distinguish a theatre from the street it is in: the Whitehall (a theatre), Whitehall (a street).

**Museums and galleries**, for example: the British Museum, the National Gallery.

*...two works recently acquired by <u>the Tate Gallery</u>, London.*
*The original is in <u>the British Museum</u>.*

The following groups of proper nouns typically have no article:

**Stations and airports**, for example: Heathrow (Airport), Euston (Station).

*...in the train on the way to <u>Euston</u>.*
*<u>Heathrow</u> is to be expanded through a fourth terminal.*

**Schools, colleges and universities**, for example: Manchester Grammar School, Dartmouth College, Cambridge University, Kent State University.

*...a physical education student at <u>Carnegie College</u>.*
*...ecology graduates from <u>Edinburgh University</u>.*

There are many universities which are referred to with expressions including 'of', and these have the definite article, for example: the University of Wales; but if abbreviated there is no article: UCLA (the University of California at Los Angeles). Many universities have both possibilities: London University, the University of London (which is the official name).

*...filmed by scientists at <u>the University of Chicago</u>.*

**Churches, cathedrals and abbeys**, for example: St Peter's, Canterbury Cathedral, Westminster Abbey.

*...and later they were confirmed in <u>Westminster Abbey</u>.*
*It was proposed to pull down <u>Chartres Cathedral</u>.*

But with abbeys named after religious orders, and with those followed by 'of', there is a definite article: the Dominican Abbey, the Abbey of Cluny.

**Note** When you refer back to a particular building, you can use the definite article in front of the word for the building, which keeps its capital letter.

*And so round to the north side of <u>the Cathedral</u>.*

▶ Exercise 3


## 7.5 Names of streets and roads

Names of streets, roads and squares tend to have no article, for example: Oxford Street, Charing Cross Road, Park Lane, Broadway, Pennsylvania Avenue.

*Turn right off <u>Broadway</u> into <u>Caxton Street</u>.*
*It lies between <u>Leicester Square</u> on the south and <u>Oxford Street</u> on the north.*
*...second-hand bookshops in <u>Charing Cross Road</u>.*

There are a number of exceptions to this, for example: the High Street (in any town), and two streets in London: the Mall, the Strand. Certain roads can have the definite article or no article: (the) Edgware Road, (the) Old Kent Road.

*...with <u>the Mall</u> on the north and Birdcage Walk on the south.*
*She followed them along <u>the Edgware Road</u>.*

Highways and motorways tend to have the definite article, for example: the A1, the M1, the New Jersey Turnpike.

*<u>The M1</u> was down to a single lane in places.*

Names of foreign streets and squares tend to keep the definite article if there is one in the original language: the Via Veneto, the Reperbahn, the Boulevard St Michel.

*...one situated in <u>the Place Vendôme</u> and the other in <u>the Rue Cambon</u>.*

**Note** When street names are parts of addresses, the definite article sometimes can and sometimes must be left out: '24 (the) High Street', '104 Edgware Road'. The definite article is not used in street signs.

▶ Exercise 3


## 7.6 Names of ships, trains, and spacecraft

The names of ships usually have the definite article: the Titanic, the Queen Elizabeth, the Exxon Valdez.

*...and eventually <u>the Queen Elizabeth</u> put to sea.*

The names of smaller boats usually have no article.

*The front runner will undoubtedly be Richard Matthews's converted America's Cup 12-metre yacht, <u>Crusader.</u>*

Established train services have the definite article: the Orient Express.

Spacecraft tend to have no article: Challenger, Apollo 17.

## 7.7 Names of sporting events

Names of sporting events usually have the definite article: the Superbowl, the Olympic Games, the World Cup, the Cup Final, the Boat Race, the Grand National, the British Open, and so on.

*...events like <u>the World Championship</u> and <u>the Olympic Games</u>.*

You can pick out one particular case of such an event by using the definite or indefinite article: 'I've never been to a Cup Final'.

Names which are taken from the place where the event occurs do not have the definite article: Wimbledon (for tennis), Ascot and Epsom (for horse-racing events), Henley (for rowing).

*...Centre Court seats for <u>Wimbledon</u>, boxes for <u>Ascot</u>.*

▶ Exercise 4

## 7.8 Names of festivals

Names of religious and other festivals have no article: Christmas, Easter, Lent, Carnival, Corpus Christi, Ramadan, Midsummer's Day, Mother's Day, New Year's Day, St Valentine's Day, and so on. (But note the 4th of July.)

*<u>Easter</u> is a great time in Poland.*
*...the last two weeks of <u>Lent</u>.*

But you can pick out one particular event by using the definite or indefinite article.

*...the rare luxury of <u>a Christmas</u> at home.*

(For names of months and days of the week, see section 6.10.)

▶ Exercise 4

## 7.9 Names of organizations

Some names of organizations have the definite article, and some have no article.

Names of well-known organizations typically have the definite article, and they keep it when they are abbreviated: the United Nations (the UN), the BBC, the Labour Party, the FBI, the EC.

*The Labour Party has a job to do.*
*The TUC runs ten-day courses all over the country.*
*The BBC never reported my speeches.*
*...the role of the UN during the election period.*
*...something to do with the United Nations.*

If an abbreviation is pronounced as a word, then there is no article. So 'the Organization of Petroleum Exporting Countries' is usually called 'OPEC' /əʊpek/. Other examples are 'NATO' /neɪtəʊ/ and 'UNICEF' /juːnɪsef/.

*...as a member of NATO.*

Some names of charities do not have the definite article: Oxfam, Christian Aid, Mencap.

You usually refer to businesses and chains of shops with no article: General Motors, Sony, Woolworths, Shell, Nissan, Singapore Airlines.

*You could have gone to Woolworths.*
*Now Collins have brought it out in a new translation.*

This applies even when an abbreviation is used which is not pronounced as a word: BP /biːpiː/ (British Petroleum), KLM, BA, ICI, IBM and so on.

*...corporations like IBM, RCA and Xerox.*

However, if a word like 'company' is used, then the definite article is used: the Bell Telephone Company. You can find alternatives like: 'General Electric' and 'GEC' as well as 'the General Electric Company'.

▶ Exercise 5

## 7.10 Names of newspapers and periodicals

Names of newspapers published in English tend to have the definite article, including almost all the British national daily newspapers: the Times, the Guardian, the Independent, the Daily Telegraph, the Financial Times, the Daily Mail, the Daily Mirror, the Sun, the Star; the one exception is: Today.

*...the city editor of the Washington Post.*
*...in an article in the Times.*

You do not use **the** with the names of foreign newspapers: Pravda, Le Monde, Der Spiegel.

*...a long and thoughtful article in <u>Le Monde</u>.*

Names of periodicals such as magazines and journals have either the definite article or no article: Punch, Newsweek, ELT Journal, the Journal of American Psychology, the Spectator.

*...a collection of tales which previously appeared in <u>Punch.</u>*
*...a cartoon in <u>the Spectator</u>.*

▶ Exercise 6

## 7.11 Names of political institutions

The names of most political or government bodies and institutions have the definite article: the House of Commons, the House of Lords, the House of Representatives, the Senate, the Department of Trade and Industry, the State Department, the Cabinet.

*It was defeated in <u>the House of Commons</u> on 13 December.*
*Look at the percentage of lawyers in <u>the Senate.</u>*

This is true also of foreign institutions, translated or not: the Bundestag, the Dail, the Supreme Court, the Finance Ministry, the Ministry of the Interior, and so on.

*...at a special meeting of <u>the Bundestag</u>.*
*...regular briefings by <u>the Interior Ministry</u> and <u>the Foreign Ministry</u>.*

Exceptions to this are: Parliament (but the Houses of Parliament), Congress, and names of councils: Kent County Council, Leeds City Council.

*...when I was elected to <u>Parliament</u> in 1964.*
*He attended <u>Congress</u> only nine times.*

Names of locations and buildings that are used to refer metaphorically to political institutions stay as they are: Whitehall, Westminster, Downing Street, Washington, the Kremlin.

*But the final decision may be made in <u>the Kremlin</u>.*

▶ Exercise 7

## 7.12 Names of musical groups

Names of musical groups can have either no article or the definite article: Queen, the Beatles, Dire Straits, the Supremes, Fleetwood Mac. The choice of name depends on the group, and so it is possible to deliberately break ordinary rules of article usage for stylistic reasons. However, most plurals still have the definite article, for example: the Rolling Stones, the Shadows, the Eurythmics, the Doors.

*In our own time the Rolling Stones have developed a similar reputation.*
*...the gigantic commercial success of the Beatles.*

## 7.13 Personal names

The names of people usually have no article: John Smith, Mary Jones. This is true no matter how someone's name is given: Smith, J. Smith, John F. Smith, Mr Smith, Dr Smith, Dr J.F. Smith, Captain Smith, Lord Smith, and so on.

*Margaret Thatcher is doing more than enough of that already.*
*...the victory of Mrs Thatcher in the 1979 election.*
*As the riots continued Thatcher came under pressure.*

There are a number of situations where the definite article is necessary. It is used when you are referring to a family by making the name plural: the Wilsons, the Masons.

*...and everyone will see how crude the Swansons really are.*

You can stress the definite article with names of people to mean someone famous: 'I met Paul McCartney the other day.' 'You mean *the* Paul McCartney?'

*...before I could assure her that I was not one of the Schuylers.*

(See section 1.4 for how to pronounce 'the' in this situation; see section 4.14 for another situation where it is stressed.)

The definite article is used in certain titles: the Reverend John Collins, the Prince of Wales (but Prince Charles), the Duke of Westminster, the Countess of Harewood. It is also used in the descriptive names of some monarchs: William the Conqueror, Ivan the Terrible, Alfred the Great.

The indefinite article can be used with personal names, where it means something like 'a certain', or 'someone called...'.

*...the librarian, a Mrs Willard.*
*I explained that a Mr George Cole, with whom I was currently acting, had damaged it.*

The speaker or writer is suggesting that the reader or listener does not know the person.

The indefinite article can also be used with a family name to pick out one member.

*If there were always an England there would always be <u>a
Rothermere</u>.*

(See section 7.14 for more instances where personal nouns are used
with the definite and indefinite articles.)

▶ Exercise 8

## 7.14 Converting proper nouns

We saw in sections 7.7, 7.8, and 7.13 cases where proper nouns
could be (unusually) used with the indefinite article. However,
there are many cases where you can use the indefinite article, and
by extension the definite article, with what appear to be proper
nouns. In fact, what is happening is that these nouns are being
used as common nouns instead of proper nouns (see section 7.1 for
the difference), even though the capital letter remains. This is
similar to the process of conversion that was described in Chapter
2. With converted proper nouns you can talk about particular
instances using the definite or indefinite articles; the noun can also
be plural.

There are a number of predictable ways in which you use
converted proper nouns. You use a converted proper noun:

● when you want to suggest that someone or something is similar
to someone or something famous: 'She's a proper Shakespeare',
'the buying power of an IBM'.

*He is the nearest we have to <u>an English Leonardo da Vinci</u>.*
*Your son could be <u>another Einstein</u>.*

● when you are talking about a copy or instance of something,
especially a newspaper or magazine: 'a Times' means 'a copy of the
Times'.

*He bought <u>a Daily Gleaner</u> and returned to his place.*

● when you are referring to a product or a work by someone, for
example a car produced by a particular manufacturer, or a
painting by a famous painter.

*The trip had taken two days in <u>the shiny new Ford</u>.*
*Would I recognise <u>a Renoir</u>?*

Sometimes a trademark for a product is used for all products of the
same kind. For example, many people would call any vacuum
cleaner a 'Hoover', though 'Hoover' is a trademark for one
particular make.

● when you want to talk about one branch of a shop or business.

*...to make room for <u>the new Woolworth's</u>.*

● when you want to pick out a particular 'version' of something: 'This isn't the London I used to know'.

*...if there were always <u>an England</u>.*

▶ Exercise 9

# 8 Articles in the noun group

## 8.1 Introduction: the noun group

Most of the previous chapters have looked at how to decide whether you need an article or not, and whether it should be the definite or indefinite article. This chapter looks at what to do with an article when you have decided that it is necessary. It deals with such questions as:

● where to place an article in the noun group;
● which words can be combined with articles and which words cannot;
● when you can leave out articles for structural reasons.

We will also look at some more cases where the definite article is used without a noun.

Articles occur as part of noun groups. A **noun group** is a group of words based around a head, which is usually a noun. The diagram below shows how a noun group is divided up.

| DETERMINER | MODIFIER | HEAD | QUALIFIER |
|------------|----------|------|-----------|
| the | tall | girl | with black hair |

As you can see, the articles, along with other determiners, belong in the first part of a noun group; they are discussed in section 8.2 below. In the second part, the modifier, you usually find adjectives like 'tall', but nouns can also be used here; this is dealt with in section 8.6 below. The third part, the head, is usually a noun, but we have seen cases in section 5.5 where this can be an adjective, and there are other cases in sections 8.9 and 8.10 below. The last part, the qualifier, is usually made up of a phrase, as we saw in sections 4.9 and 4.10.

The only essential part in a noun group is the head; in some cases the determiner is also necessary, but the other parts are optional. There are a number of types of noun which can be used on their own in a noun group:

● count nouns in the plural, as in section 2.2
...*so she drank coffee and smoked <u>cigarettes</u>.*

● uncount nouns, as in section 2.3
...*so she drank <u>coffee</u> and smoked cigarettes.*

● plural nouns, as in section 2.5
...*the shop that deals only in <u>trousers</u>.*

● many proper nouns, as in Chapter 7

*...long before I entered <u>Parliament</u>.*

There are also nouns which must have a determiner in normal circumstances:

● count nouns in the singular, as in section 2.2

*They sat on the grass under <u>a tree</u>.*

● so-called 'unique' nouns, which need the definite article, as in section 4.8 (although this is not an absolute rule)

*...the highest material living standards in <u>the world</u>.*

● many proper nouns, which need the definite article, as in Chapter 7

*...anywhere in <u>the UK</u>.*


## 8.2 Combining articles with other determiners

Determiners include the articles, possessive determiners ('my', 'your', and so on), demonstratives ('this', 'that', 'these', 'those'), words indicating quantity ('all', 'some', 'few', 'several', 'many', and so on), and numbers ('one', 'two', and so on).

*...a birthday lunch with <u>my</u> mother.*
*Many of <u>these</u> ideas are already being tested.*
*<u>Some</u> success had been achieved.*

  **WARNING**   It is possible to have more than one determiner in a noun group, but there are many combinations which are not possible. In particular, you cannot combine the articles with possessive determiners ('my', 'your', and so on); you cannot say 'a my friend' or 'the my friend'. However, you can say 'a friend of mine'. Possessive determiners already have the idea of uniqueness suggested by 'the', so it is wrong to use both together.

*Gerhard is <u>a friend of mine</u>.*

**Note** Words indicating quantity which cannot be combined directly with the definite article can be used as pronouns in front of 'of' and the definite article: 'some of the money'.

*...to talk to <u>some of the</u> young people.*

▶ Exercise 2


## 8.3 Combining determiners with the definite article

The definite article can have a determiner in front of it and after it.

*Many people don't think of <u>all the other</u> things that can happen.*

Determiners which can come in front of the definite article are 'all', 'both', 'half', multipliers like 'twice', 'double', 'three times' and so on, and fractions like 'two-thirds'. These are sometimes called **predeterminers**.

*This will provide all the information you need.*
*...with the consent of both the establishments concerned.*
*...an area half the size of a football pitch.*
*...a house worth almost three times the price paid for the first house.*
*Give one-third the usual amount.*

'All', 'both' and 'half' have alternatives with 'of', with little or no difference in meaning.

*...conforming to all of the rules. (all the rules)*
*...and both of the MPs turned up. (both the MPs)*
*Half of the remainder will be divided. (half the remainder)*

Don't forget that 'all' and 'both' can be used in front of a noun without the definite article.

*The Social Democratic Party continues to see itself as all things to all people.*
*Both girls were attractive and intelligent.*

A number of determiners can come after the definite article; here is a list of them.

| | | |
|---|---|---|
| few | many | other |
| little | one | several |

*...the few letters he wrote to me at school.*
*...on the other hand.*
*...the one outfit I have never purchased.*
*...among the many difficult problems before him.*
*She was taken the several miles south to her home.*

The definite article occurs in front of other numbers as well as 'one'.

*...the role of local governments in the three countries.*
*...based on the difference between the two.*

▶ Exercises 1 and 2

## 8.4 Combining determiners with the indefinite article

The indefinite article can have a determiner in front of it or after it. Determiners which can occur before the indefinite article are 'half', 'many', 'quite', 'rather', 'such' and 'what' (with an idea of exclamation).

*...half a cup of cold coffee.*
*I've spent many a moonlit night here.*
*Countless numbers of workers are being faced with such a choice.*
*What a horrible idea!*

The indefinite article can also occur in front of 'half' (which is then an adjective); compare these two sentences.

*...cutting a half hour from prime time.*
*For half an hour the room was quiet.*

But it is more common to put the indefinite article after 'half', especially in British English.

The only determiner which can follow the indefinite article as part of a noun group is 'other'; the combination is always written as one word: 'another'.

*Would you like another pint?*

Don't forget that the indefinite article is also found in numbers like 'a dozen', 'a hundred', 'a thousand', and so on. (See section 3.5.)

▶ Exercise 2

## 8.5 'A few' and 'a little'

The two determiners 'a few' and 'a little' are regarded as one unit, not as combinations involving the indefinite article. This is because they don't behave like the indefinite article: 'a few' occurs with nouns in the plural, and 'a little' occurs with uncount nouns.

*He stands for a few minutes on the porch.*
*It obviously takes a little time.*

In addition, the difference in meaning between 'few' and 'a few' cannot be explained by the addition of the indefinite article. 'Few' emphasizes that there are only a small number of things; 'a few' just indicates that there are a small number of things.

There is clearly a difference between the determiner 'a little', as in 'We need a little luck', and a combination of the indefinite article and the adjective 'little' (= 'small'), as in 'a little girl'.

*I used to go there when I was a little girl.*

'A little' can also be an adverb meaning something like 'slightly'.

*We must look a little more closely.*

## 8.6 Nouns as modifiers

One of the most important factors in using articles is the type of noun that the article goes with; Chapters 2, 6 and 7 have looked at different aspects of this. However, in many sentences nouns are used not as the head of a noun group, but as modifiers, like adjectives (see section 8.1); and these nouns do not influence the choice of article in front of them. So it is important to recognise when a noun is acting as a head and when it is a modifier.

Consider the following noun group:

*...a meat and vegetable stew.*

In this noun group there are two nouns acting as modifiers ('meat' and 'vegetable') in front of the head ('stew'); 'stew' is the relevant word when choosing the indefinite article.

Proper nouns are often used as modifiers, and so you often find an article in front of a proper noun when you would not expect one, or no article where you would.

*...at a Congress fringe meeting today.*
*...a Times reporter.*
*The London line began ringing.*
*Water wheels were pumping Thames water to the City.*

'Congress' and 'London' are proper nouns usually used with no article; 'Times' and 'Thames' usually need the definite article. But here they are all modifiers and the article in front of them applies to the whole noun group.

▶ Exercise 3


## 8.7 Word order with 'so', 'how', 'too', 'as', and 'that'

Usually modifiers come after determiners (see section 8.1). But when 'so', 'how', and 'too' are used with adjectives the indefinite article (if necessary) comes after.

*Her legs, for so stout a woman, were thin.*
*Only something most unusual could have made so large a hole.*
*Now they could see how small a beast it was.*
*They know how long, how costly, and how heartbreaking a task it is.*
*But it's too good a job.*
*Politics is too important a matter to be left to experts.*

'As' and 'that', when used with adjectives, have the same effect on word order: 'It's not that big a problem'. ('That' is informal here).

*...Butcher, as inspirational a figure as Bryan Robson.*

Instead of using 'so' and 'how' you can express the same idea with 'such' and 'what' using ordinary word order: 'such a stout woman', 'such a large hole', 'what a small beast', 'what a long, costly and heartbreaking task'.

▶ Exercise 4

## 8.8 Leaving out articles

There are a number of situations when it is possible or necessary to leave out articles in front of nouns or adjectives which normally would have them. This is not the same as having no article; it is usually possible to compare these examples with sentences where either a definite or an indefinite article is used. (See section 6.14 for a similar situation.)

Articles can be left out:

● when two nouns (or adjectives), both acting as head of a noun group, are joined together with 'and' or 'or'; the second head can be without its article. This happens with both the definite and the indefinite article.

*They had enhanced the reliability and quality of radio reception.*
*...a coffee cup and saucer.*
*You can order traveller's cheques through a local bank or travel agent.*

You don't have to leave out the second article; you can say 'a coffee cup and a saucer'. But if you do leave it out, the two nouns must be closely related in meaning; you couldn't say 'There was a matchbox and jacket on the table'.

● in language which has to be shortened for reasons of space, such as telegrams, instructions, notes and newspaper headlines; a telegram message like 'Send report immediately' would mean 'Send the report immediately' or 'Send a report immediately'. Here is a typical newspaper headline.

*Ukraine divisions deepened by Party's failure to condemn coup.*

This could be read as 'The divisions in (the) Ukraine have been deepened by the Party's failure to condemn the coup'. As you can see, it is not only articles which are left out in this way.

● when nouns referring to two contrasting people or things are joined by 'and'.

*The independent allowances for husband and wife will both be available.*
*...the natural relationship between father and son.*
*...as the distinctions between employer and employee are gradually eroded.*
*There was a pause, and doctor and patient looked steadily at each other across the quiet room.*
*...with little gardens between river and road.*

Note that in this case both nouns have no article.

● in introductory phrases like 'Fact is ...', 'Thing is ...', 'Trouble is ...', 'Truth is ...'. These can all be matched to normal expressions beginning with the definite article: 'The fact is ...' and so on.

*Fact is, it's getting serious.*

This use is informal and occurs mainly in spoken English.

● with count nouns which are being used to address a person or animal (sometimes called **vocatives**).

*Good grief, man, what are you doing here?*

▶ Exercise 5

## 8.9 The definite article with adjectives meaning 'something...'

Although the head of a noun group is usually a noun, there are situations where an adjective can have this role. One case is described in section 5.5. Another case is where the definite article is used in front of an adjective to mean something with that quality. The first example below means 'People asked him to do things which were impossible'.

*People asked him the impossible.*
*Politics is the art of the possible.*
*It merely states the obvious.*
*...confused and afraid of the unknown.*

The following adjectives are often used after the definite article in this way.

| | | | | |
|---|---|---|---|---|
| bizarre | inevitable | possible | unbelievable | unthinkable |
| exotic | new | ridiculous | unexpected | |
| impossible | obvious | sublime | unknown | |
| incredible | old | supernatural | unreal | |

**Note** This use is different from that in section 5.5, where adjectives are used to refer to groups of people.

▶ Exercise 6

## 8.10 The definite article with comparative adjectives and adverbs

The definite article is used with comparative adjectives and adverbs to indicate how a difference in something involves a difference in something else.

*The simpler the motion or operation, the better the worker will perform it.*

*The more radical the change, the steeper the price.*
*The more the TUC came under attack, the stronger it grew.*

There are some fixed expressions like: 'the more the merrier'
(which usually means that you want as many people as possible),
'the sooner the better' (which means that you want something as
soon as possible), and others where the second part is '...the better'
(which mean that you want something with as much of a particular
quality as possible).

*What's one more when you already have five? The more the merrier.*
*I'd be deeply grateful if you'd let me know - the sooner the better,*
*please.*
*A doctor is pleased to answer any question that he can, the easier, the*
*better.*

You can also use the definite article in front of one comparative
adjective or adverb, especially after 'all', to emphasize that
something will affect a situation.

*You'll sleep the better for it.*
*We'll have him back here all the quicker if you co-operate with us.*
*His longing was all the more agonizing because he could speak of it*
*to no-one.*

▶ Exercise 7

# Exercises

## 1 The forms of the articles

### Exercise 1 (section 1.2)

Put the numbers in the sentences below into the correct row according to the pronunciation of 'the'. The first one has been done for you.

/ðə/: ...........................................................................................

/ði/: ...*1*......................................................................................

Get the (1) address from the (2) post-office.

Only the (3) other afternoon, climbing up from the (4) Underground, I found the (5) staircase barred.

Compare that to the (6) UK figure of about 1000 deaths.

The (7) porter at the (8) door looked a shade bleak.

He is now the (9) enemy of God as well the (10) opponent of man.

The (11) ruse is basically the (12) same as the (13) one used by Odysseus.

They lived only five minutes from the (14) university.

### Exercise 2 (section 1.3)

Complete these sentences by putting 'a' or 'an' in the spaces provided. The first one has been done for you.

1) It is always fatal to ask ...*an*... expert.

2) Secretive as ............ boy of six, secretive as ............ old man of seventy.

3) ............ brilliant young woman with ............ M.A. degree.

4) She dislikes him as ............ being, as ............ creature, as ............ appearance.

5) I prefer management on ............ one-to-one basis.

6) ............ hour ............ day would be enough.

**Exercise 3** (sections 1.2 and 1.3)

Put the following words or phrases in the correct category according to their initial sound. The first two have been done for you. When you have finished, practise saying them together with 'a', 'an', and 'the'.

| | | | |
|---|---|---|---|
| arm | hand | neck | umbrella |
| BBC | head | nose | uncle |
| ear | honest man | one-man band | uniform |
| eye | honour | toe | unit |
| FBI agent | leg | ugly man | university |
| finger | MP | UK | useful idea |

Pronounced with an initial consonant sound; use 'the' /ðə/ or 'a' /ə/:
 *BBC*
.................................................................................................

.................................................................................................

Pronounced with an initial vowel sound; use 'the' /ði/ or 'an' /ən/:
 *arm*
.................................................................................................

.................................................................................................

**Exercise 4** (sections 1.2 and 1.3)

Now practise your pronunciation of 'a', 'an', and 'the'. Below is a list of members of the family, but there is a 'typing error' in each one. Find the errors and correct them, first orally then by filling in the spaces provided. The first one has been done for you.

1) baughter: ...... *the* /ðə/ *b* ... is wrong. It should be ...... *a* /ə/ *d* ......

2) fatler: ............................. is wrong. It should be ...............................

3) simter: ............................. is wrong. It should be ...............................

4) coxsin: ............................. is wrong. It should be ...............................

5) nephey: ............................. is wrong. It should be ...............................

6) grandsin: ............................. is wrong. It should be ...............................

7) gunt: ............................. is wrong. It should be ...............................

8) farents: ............................. is wrong. It should be ...............................

9) nitce: ............................. is wrong. It should be ...............................

10) mothen: ............................. is wrong. It should be ...............................

# 2 Articles and nouns

## Exercise 1 (sections 2.2, 2.3, and 2.4)

Look at these words; if they are count nouns, put 'a' or 'an' in front of them; if they are uncount nouns, put a dash. The first two have been done for you.

1) ............*a*............ dog
2) ............–............ wool
3) ..................... book
4) ..................... advice
5) ..................... information
6) ..................... idea
7) ..................... trip
8) ..................... sand
9) ..................... shopping
10) ..................... trouble

11) .....................remark
12) ..................... hatred
13) ..................... job
14) ..................... water
15) ..................... furniture
16) ..................... problem
17) ..................... music
18) ..................... anger
19) ..................... travel
20) ..................... news

## Exercise 2 (section 2.4)

The sentences below all contain nouns in the plural. Some can occur only in the plural form: these are plural nouns. Others can occur both in the singular and the plural form: these are count nouns. Write 'plural' in the space if the noun is a plural noun and 'count' if it is a count noun. The first one has been done for you.

1) Pass me the scissors. ....*plural*.....................................

2) When he opened it the contents fell out. .....................................

3) Dresses are more comfortable than trousers. ............. .............

4) Please send my thanks to them. .....................................

5) Put it on the scales and weigh it. .....................................

6) He took off his glasses and wiped them on his gloves. ......... .........

7) A good diet will improve your looks. .....................................

8) Last year my earnings went down. .....................................

76

**Exercise 3** (sections 2.7 and 2.8)

Decide whether the converted uncount nouns in the following sentences should be understood as 'a unit of' or 'a type of'. Write 'type' or 'unit' in the space provided. The first one has been done for you.

1) There were many beers on sale at the festival. ......*type*......................

2) Every year she makes four jams. ....................................................

3) In each pack there are six Cokes. ...................................................

4) Be careful. That's your third coffee this morning. ...........................

5) New plastics are constantly coming on the market. .........................

6) They serve good soups and meat in red wine. ..................................

7) In British pubs you don't usually ask for 'a beer'. ............................

8) Personally, I prefer the teas of India. .............................................

9) Three sugars, please. ...................................................................

10) The best whiskies come from Scotland. ..........................................

**Exercise 4** (sections 2.6, 2.7, 2.8, and 2.11)

In the expressions below decide if you can cross out the two middle words and in this way convert an uncount noun to a count noun. If you can, write 'yes'. If you cannot, write 'no'. The first one has been done for you.

1) a cup of coffee ......*yes*..................

2) a pair of scissors ............................

3) a piece of string ............................

4) a sort of cheese ............................

5) a bit of chalk ............................

6) a piece of cake ............................

7) a piece of news ............................

8) a type of beer ............................

9) an item of information ............................

10) a loaf of bread ............................

11) a lump of sugar ............................

12) a bar of soap ............................

# Exercises: 2 Articles and nouns

## Exercise 5 (section 2.8)

Look at the questions and answers below and put into each space a converted uncount noun in the plural. The first one has been done for you.

1) 'Which ...*cheeses*... do you sell?' - 'Cheddar, camembert and gouda.'

2) 'What are coffins made of?' - 'Oak, teak, and other hard ......................... .'

3) 'What ......................... are found there?' - 'Gold, silver, lead and tin.'

4) 'Which ..................... are produced in this region?' - 'A dry red and a rosé.'

5) 'Which ......................... do you sell?' - 'Tuborg, Carlsberg and Budweiser.'

## Exercise 6 (section 2.9)

Complete the following sentences with a count noun converted to an uncount noun, as in the first sentence, which has been completed for you. Choose from these words:

| bird | dog | insect | truck |
|------|-----|--------|-------|
| cat | flower | spider | vehicle |

1) Cars, lorries and buses are different kinds of ...*vehicle*............... .

2) Ducks are a type of ......................................................... .

3) Bees, ants and mosquitoes are varieties of ...................................... .

4) Alsatians are a breed of ............................................................ .

5) Lions and tigers are both types of big ........................................ .

6) Roses and carnations are types of ................................................ .

## Exercise 7 (section 2.10)

Complete the definitions below, choosing from the words in the box, together with 'a' where needed. The first one has been done for you.

| faith | glass | memory | reason | rubber | study |
|-------|-------|--------|--------|--------|-------|
| a faith | a glass | a memory | a reason | a rubber | a study |

1) ......*Memory*..... is the faculty which we use to remember.

2) ..................... is the process of learning actively.

3) ..................... is a cause or explanation for something.

4) ..................... is something we use to erase or remove a mistake.

5) ..................... is a set of beliefs like a religion.

6) ..................... is something remembered.

7) ..................... is a substance used for making tyres and other objects.

8) ..................... is having confidence in, or believing in, something.

9) ..................... is a room where people can read or work quietly.

10) ..................... is the process of working things out rationally.

## Exercise 8 (section 2.10)

In the following sentences, the underlined nouns can be count or uncount depending on their meaning. Decide which meaning is being used in each sentence, and cross out the incorrect noun group. The first one has been done for you.

1) To press clothes you need ~~iron~~/an iron.

2) Language/A language is unique to humans.

3) In her youth she was beauty/a beauty.

4) We are looking for people with experience/an experience.

5) He kept his money in tin/a tin under the bed.

6) She's been looking for work/a work for ages.

7) You should study law/a law at university.

8) Then everybody called for him to make speech/a speech.

9) Play/A play is more natural for children than adults.

10) Charity/A charity begins at home.

## Exercise 9 (section 2.11)

Put one of these counting expressions in front of each of the uncount nouns below. There may be more than one possibility. The first one has been done for you.

a drop of    a grain of    a lump of    an item of    a pair of    a piece of

1) ...*a drop of*... water

2) ........................... sugar

3) ........................... iron

4) ........................... scissors

5) ........................... music

6) ........................... news

7) ........................... shorts

8) ........................... meat

9) ........................... rice

10) ........................... research

11) ........................... information

12) ........................... sand

# 3 Using the indefinite article

**Exercise 1** (sections 3.2 and 3.3)

Look at the noun groups underlined in the sentences below. Where you think the speaker or writer is familiar with the items referred to, complete the sentences by putting 'it' in the spaces provided. Where you think the writer or reader is not familiar with the items referred to, put 'one'. The first one has been done for you.

1) I'm looking for <u>an atlas</u>. Do you know where I can get ......*one*......?

2) I've lost <u>a button</u>. I don't suppose I'll ever find ................................. .

3) Our son wants <u>a bicycle</u> but I don't think he should have ................ yet.

4) 'Here's <u>a hundred pounds</u>.' - 'Thanks, but I won't need ..................... .'

5) I bought <u>a new television</u> last week but my wife doesn't like ................ .

6) 'Would you like <u>a beer</u>?' - 'Yes, I'd love ............................................. .'

7) She wants <u>a new car</u> but he says they don't need ............................... .

**Exercise 2** (section 3.4)

Complete the answers to the questions below. Together with 'a' or 'an', use these words:

| | | |
|---|---|---|
| artist | explorer | playwright |
| cartoon character | film star | scientist |
| composer | philosopher | writer |

The first one has been done for you.

1) Who was Shakespeare? He was .....*a playwright*............................ .

2) Who was Mozart? He was ................................................................. .

3) Who was Einstein? He was ............................................................... .

4) Who is Meryl Streep? She's ............................................................. .

5) Who is Mickey Mouse? He's ............................................................ .

6) Who was Marco Polo? He was ......................................................... .

7) Who was Leonardo da Vinci? He was ............................................. .

8) Who was Confucius? He was ........................................................... .

9) Who was Tolstoy? He was ............................................................... .

## Exercise 3 (section 3.5)

Look at these sentences. Decide if you can replace 'one' with 'a' without changing the meaning, putting 'yes' or 'no' in the spaces provided. The first one has been done for you.

1) It measured one quarter of an inch. ......*yes*....

2) The distance is one kilometre, four hundred metres. ..................

3) 5110; that's five thousand, one hundred and ten. ..................

4) He drank one coffee and two orange juices. ..................

5) There's only one thing we need now. ..................

Now, with these sentences, decide if you can replace 'a' with 'one'.

6) I only asked for half a kilo. ..................

7) He works eighty hours a week. ..................

8) The river is a mile wide. ..................

9) That seems a good idea. ..................

10) A millimetre is a thousandth of a metre. ............... ............... ...............

## Exercise 4 (section 3.6)

Work out these simple problems. The first one has been done for you.

1) The plums were ............*40p a kilo*............................... , so I bought two kilos for 80p.

2) The plane flew 1,800 miles in three hours at a speed of ...........................
   ............................................... .

3) His annual salary is $30,000, so he earns ...................................
   ............................................... .

4) The meetings are held ........................................................ ,
   every Monday and Thursday.

5) A five-day forty-hour working week means on average ...........................
   ............................................... .

6) We travelled twenty kilometres in fifteen minutes, so our speed was
   ............................................... .

# 4 Specific uses of the definite article

## Exercise 1 (sections 4.2 and 4.3)

Complete the story below by inserting 'a' or 'the' in the spaces as required. The first one has been done for you.

Once upon a time, there was (1) ....*a*..... cat and (2) ............ dog who lived in (3) ............ small house. One day (4) ............ cat said to (5) ............ dog, 'This place is too small for us - we need (6) ............ bigger house.' (7) ............ dog agreed. 'We could even have (8) ............ garden where I could bury my bones.' 'Well I'm not sure (9) ............ garden is a good idea,' said (10) ............ cat. 'Who would cut the grass?' 'We could employ (11) ............ cat to do it,' said (12) ............ dog. 'Why not (13) ............ dog?' said (14) ............ cat. And so they never left (15) ............ small house because they couldn't agree.

## Exercise 2 (section 4.3)

Look at the instructions for making scrambled eggs below and decide which form of the noun group is correct: the basic noun without an article, the noun with 'the', or a pronoun ('it' or 'them'). Cross out the incorrect noun groups. The first one has been done for you.

To make scrambled eggs you need (1) ~~eggs/the eggs/them~~, (2) milk/the milk/it and (3) butter/the butter/it. Cut a slice of (4) butter/the butter/it and put (5) butter/the butter/it into a heated saucepan. Next pour (6) milk/the milk/it over (7) butter/the butter/it. Then break (8) eggs/the eggs/them and pour (9) eggs/the eggs/them into the pan. Season to taste and stir quickly until everything is solid.

## Exercise 3 (section 4.4)

Decide whether the two nouns underlined in each sentence refer to the same thing or not. If you can change the second noun group to 'it', 'him', or 'her' without changing the meaning, the two nouns do refer to the same thing. This is true of the first sentence, which has been done for you. (It could equally be '...so how do you know it so well?') Write 'same' or 'different' in the spaces provided.

1) You've never been to <u>London</u> before so how do you know the <u>place</u> so well? .........*same*.........

2) I can't understand this <u>text</u>; the <u>language</u> is very difficult. ......................

3) My parents bought me a <u>piano</u> but I don't like the <u>thing</u>. ........................

4) When I switched on your <u>dishwasher</u>, the <u>machine</u> made a loud noise.

   ............................

5) My <u>car</u> has broken down again. I'll have to check the <u>engine</u>. .................

6) What do you think of the <u>director</u>? Personally I can't stand the <u>woman</u>.

   ............................

## Exercise 4 (section 4.5)

Complete the sentences below putting 'the' in each space, together with a noun that is associated with the noun which is underlined. The first one has been done for you.

1) We went into <u>shops</u> which had absolutely nothing on ...*the shelves*... .

2) You shouldn't ask a <u>question</u> if you already know ........................... .

3) I've never taught a <u>class</u> where ...................................... are so lazy.

4) It was a lovely <u>house</u> but ..................... were too steep for old people.

5) In a <u>test</u> ............................... should not be too difficult or too easy.

6) It's a <u>newspaper</u> where ........................ aren't covered with pictures.

7) I'm not surprised you can't walk in those <u>shoes</u>. ...............................
   are much too high.

8) Before you go on a long journey in your <u>car</u>, check to make sure

   ....................................... have enough air in them.

9) I bought the <u>radio</u> in a sale. ........................ had been slashed by 50%.

10) What's the point in buying an expensive <u>television</u> if ........................
    isn't clear?

## Exercise 5 (section 4.5)

Complete these sentences with words appropriate to the situation. The first space has been filled for you.

The room was completely empty so some of us sat down on ...*the floor*...
while others leaned against .......................................... . It was hot so I tried to

open .......................................... ; they were stuck. It started getting dark so I

turned on .......................................... ; it didn't work. Then we realised that

.......................................... was locked.

# Exercises: 4 Specific uses of the definite article

## Exercise 6 (section 4.6)

Find and link each sentence in the column on the left with a suitable situation on the right. The first one has been done for you.

| | | | |
|---|---|---|---|
| 1) | Could we have the menu, please? | a) | in a garden |
| 2) | The music isn't very good, is it? | b) | in a living room |
| 3) | I hope the film is going to be good. | c) | at a wedding |
| 4) | Ow! The sand is really hot. | d) | in a classroom |
| 5) | Doesn't the bride look beautiful? | e) | in a restaurant |
| 6) | Switch on the television. | f) | on a beach |
| 7) | The judge has fallen asleep. | g) | in a cinema queue |
| 8) | The grass needs cutting. | h) | in a bathroom |
| 9) | Where's the soap? | i) | in a courtroom |
| 10) | Who's been writing on the blackboard? | j) | at a concert |

## Exercise 7 (section 4.7)

Look at the map of the small town of Theaton on the opposite page. Complete the questions and answers about the town below, using 'a', 'an', or 'the' as required. The first one has been done for you.

1) 'Where is _the police station_?' - 'It's on Duke Street.'

2) 'Where does Park Avenue begin?' - 'At ..................................... .'

3) 'Where is the library?' - 'It's right next to ..................................... .'

4) 'What important buildings are situated on Green Street?' -
   '..................................... and ..................................... .'

5) 'Where is ..................................... ?' - 'On Field Street, opposite
   ..................................... .'

6) 'What's that building near ..................................... ?' - 'That's
   the hotel.'

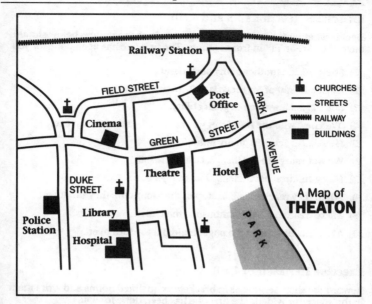

A Map of **THEATON**

CHURCHES
STREETS
RAILWAY
BUILDINGS

Railway Station
FIELD STREET
Post Office
Cinema
GREEN STREET
Theatre
Hotel
PARK AVENUE
DUKE STREET
Library
Police Station
Hospital
PARK

## Exercise 8 (section 4.8)

Complete the sentences below by inserting 'the', 'a', 'an', or – into the spaces provided, according to whether or not the noun is referring to something generally seen as unique in the given context. The first one has been done for you.

1) People have always wanted to be able to fly like birds in ...*the*... sky.

2) Every solar system has ............ sun.

3) ............ equator runs round the middle of ............ earth.

4) It was given to Spain by ............ Pope in the Middle Ages.

5) Can you imagine ............ world with no wars, no hunger, no pain?

6) There's nowhere on ............ earth like Hong Kong.

7) When ............ moon passes between ............ sun and the earth, it is called an eclipse.

8) That night there was ............ amazing sky, full of different colours.

9) It's the oldest university in ............ world.

10) We don't know how old ............ universe is.

85

## Exercises: 4 Specific uses of the definite article

### Exercise 9 (sections 4.9 and 4.10)

Decide whether the qualified noun groups in the sentences below should have 'the', 'a', or 'an' in front of them. The first one has been done for you.

1) She's ...*the*... mother of my best friend.

2) ............ height of Mt Blanc is 4807 metres.

3) She's ............ woman of great ability.

4) We knew who the murderer was at ............ end of the first act.

5) He's ............ cousin on my father's side.

6) We were surprised at ............ size of the bill.

7) Many children have ............ fear of rejection.

8) When they reached ............ top of the mountain, they sat down.

9) There was ............ dead mouse in the corner.

10) At ............ bottom of the page it said 'Please turn over'.

### Exercise 10 (section 4.10)

Reword the short sentences in brackets as qualified nouns and write them in the spaces provided. The first one has been done for you.

1) (The stars arrived.) Crowds watched *the arrival of the stars* .

2) (The shop was opened.) ............................ was followed by a party.

3) (A boy has disappeared.) Police are worried about ............................
......................................................................................... .

4) (He lost all his money.) He never recovered after ............................ .

5) (A baby girl was born.) They were delighted with ............................
......................................................................................... .

6) (The painting exists.) No one knew about ............................
......................................................................................... .

7) (The city will be destroyed.) Nothing can be done to stop ...................
......................................................................................... .

8) (The body was discovered.) An extensive search led to ........................
......................................................................................... .

9) (The rebels were defeated.) ............................................................
......................................................... meant the end of the war.

## Exercise 11 (section 4.11)

Fill in the gaps in these sentences using the superlative form of an adjective. The first one has been done for you.

1) Elephants are .......*the largest*....................... land animals.

2) Diamond is ........................................ substance known to man.

3) Kilimanjaro is ................................................ mountain in Africa.

4) The Volga is .......................................................... river in Europe.

5) .................................................... man in the world weighs 32 stone.

6) Mercury is .......................................................... planet to the sun.

7) ................................................ woman in Britain was 114 recently.

## Exercise 12 (section 4.12)

Complete the sentences below, using the adjectives from the list; some have to be used more than once. Be careful - there is at least one sentence which requires 'a' rather than 'the'. The first sentence has been completed for you.

first   last   next   only   right   same   wrong

1) Neil Armstrong was .......*the first*................. man on the moon.

2) 'I'm sorry I'm late. I caught .................................. bus.' - 'Well in future try to catch .................................. one.'

3) What a coincidence! We live in .................................. street.

4) I'm warning you! .................................. person who does that will be in trouble!

5) He was .................................. survivor of the crash; everyone else died.

6) There isn't always .................................. way of doing things.

7) He waited until .................................. possible moment, then jumped.

8) Joanne hasn't changed; she's .................................. as ever.

9) Before leaving, he had .................................. look around the house.

10) What a surprise! You're .................................. person I expected to see.

# 5 Articles with generic reference

## Exercise 1 (section 5.2)

Look at the sentences below. Decide whether the noun groups underlined refer generically to something or refer to something in particular, and write 'generic' or 'particular' in the spaces provided. Try making them plural; if there is no change in meaning, they are generic. In the first one, which has been done for you, the meaning of the sentence could be expressed as 'Streams are small rivers'.

1) A stream is a small river. ......*generic*.........................

2) An undertaker was arrested for drunken driving. ...........................

3) The best pet for a child is a dog. ..............................

4) If you don't like public transport, you should get a car. ........................

5) A dog is sitting listening to a record-player. ...........................

6) You can never trust a politician. ...........................

7) A car isn't the best way to travel in a city. ...........................

## Exercise 2 (section 5.2)

Try to complete these definitions; they have been taken from the Collins Cobuild English Language Dictionary. The first one has been done for you.

1) ......*A kitchen*...... is a room that is used for cooking.

2) .............................. is a structure that is built over a river, railway, road etc.

3) .............................. is a device. . .which you carry to protect yourself from the rain.

4) .............................. is a building in which Christians worship.

5) .............................. is an oval or rounded object produced by female birds.

6) .............................. is an institution where students study for degrees.

7) .............................. is a book in which the words of a language are listed alphabetically.

8) .............................. is a place, usually in the open air, where goods are bought and sold.

9) ................................. is a person who steals something from another person, especially without using violence.

10) ................................. is a weapon which explodes and damages or destroys a large area.

## Exercise 3 (section 5.3)

Answer these questions using 'the' with a singular noun. The first one has been done for you.

1) What's the tallest animal on earth? .....*the giraffe*.....................

2) What's the largest of all creatures? ...............................................

3) What animal is called 'the king of the jungle'? ...............................

4) Which is the largest of the apes? ...................................................

5) Which is the largest land animal? ...................................................

6) Which animal can have one or two humps on its back? ......................

7) Which animal is often called 'man's best friend'? ............................

## Exercise 4 (section 5.3)

Complete these formal or technical statements with 'the' and a noun. The first one has been done for you.

1) The organ which pumps blood around our bodies is called *the heart*

2) Nowadays many people keep a television in ............................... as well as in.............................. so that they can watch in bed.

3) Between the ages of one and five, ............................... learns to speak a language fluently.

4) ............................... must make sure that the patient understands what is wrong.

5) ............................... has made it possible to communicate with loved ones immediately.

6) If we want to promote learning, we must make ............................... a friendlier place, somewhere where ............................... and ............................... can cooperate.

## Exercise 5 (sections 5.1, 5.2 and 5.3)

In the sentences below, make a generalization using the word in brackets at the end. Use the most suitable pattern: a singular noun with 'a' or 'an' ('a chair'), a singular noun with 'the' ('the chair'), or a plural without an article ('chairs'). Sometimes there are two possibilities. The first one has been done for you.

1) I couldn't manage if there was a ban on .......*cars*....... . (car)

2) If the infection spreads to ....................................... it can be fatal. (heart)

3) ....................................... must never forget who he or she is writing for. (writer)

4) The invention of ....................................... was a great step in the development of transport. (wheel)

5) ....................................... isn't much fun to play with. (tortoise)

6) If we don't do something soon ....................................... will die out. (whale)

7) .......................................is for sitting on, not standing on. (chair)

## Exercise 6 (section 5.4)

Complete the following statements using 'the' and a nationality word. The first one has been done for you.

1) ....*The English*.... believe that their home is their castle.

2) ....................................... are well known for their luxury fast cars like Mercedes or BMW.

3) ....................................... are the most populous nation on earth.

4) ....................................... used to believe in gods who lived on Mount Olympus.

5) ....................................... were ruled by the Tsars until 1917.

**Exercise 7** (section 5.5)

Complete the sentences below by putting 'the' together with the most appropriate of these generic adjectives in the spaces provided. The first one has been done for you.

| blind | healthy | hungry | poor | uneducated |
|-------|---------|--------|------|------------|
| deaf | homeless | lame | rich | unemployed |

1) *The unemployed* are people who have no job.

2) ........................ are people who are not sick.

3) ........................ are people who have difficulty walking.

4) ........................ are people who have a lot of money.

5) ........................ are people who cannot see.

6) ........................ are people who have very little money.

7) ........................ are people who cannot hear.

8) ........................ are people who have not had an education.

9) ........................ are people who do not have enough food to eat.

10) ........................ are people who have nowhere to live.

# 6 Article use with certain groups of words

## Exercise 1 (section 6.2)

Complete the sentences below using 'a', 'an', 'the', or – (no article) using these words. You will need to use some of the words more than once. The first one has been done for you.

newspaper  papers  phone  post  radio  telephone  television

1) If you go sailing you should listen to weather reports on ...*the radio*... .

2) Children spend too much time watching ................................................ .

3) The Times is ................................................ with a long tradition.

4) Before the days of television, people used to listen to ........................... .

5) Nowadays it's possible to buy ................................................ which you can speak into without lifting the receiver.

6) We bought ................................................ with a 21-inch screen.

7) This letter is for you; it came in ................................................ this morning.

8) I'll send you a letter; it's best not to talk about such things on

................................................ .

9) Don't believe everything you read in ................................................ .

## Exercise 2 (section 6.3)

In the sentences below, only one of the underlined noun groups is appropriate. Cross out the one that is wrong. The first one has been done for you.

1) A train/The train would be best; it leaves every hour.

2) Since they built the bridge no one uses a ferry/the ferry any more.

3) Next year you'll be able to go by hovercraft; they're starting a new service. It'll be much quicker than a boat/the boat.

4) You'll have no trouble getting home; a bus/the bus doesn't stop running till midnight.

5) There are many ways for tourists to get around London. If you don't mind travelling in tunnels, take an underground/the underground; if you like to see where you're going, sit on the top deck of a bus/the bus; and if you're in a hurry, take a taxi/the taxi.

## Exercise 3 (section 6.4)

In the sentences below, only one of the underlined noun groups is appropriate. Cross out the one that is wrong. The first one has been done for you.

1) He was a supreme master of ballet/~~a ballet~~.

2) She has returned to a theatre/the theatre after an absence of five years.

3) Our lives are dominated by television/a television.

4) This town is boring. What we need is a cinema/the cinema.

5) 'You're dressed up.' - 'Yes, we're going to opera/the opera.'

6) Film/The film is both a respected art form and a form of mass entertainment.

7) 'What can we do tonight?' - 'Well, we could go to movies/the movies.'

## Exercise 4 (section 6.5)

In the sentences below, only one of the underlined noun groups is appropriate. Cross out the one that is wrong. The first one has been done for you.

1) Both of them found work in ~~hospital~~/the hospital.

2) She could not imagine people going to church/the church looking so dull and unhappy.

3) The door was closed when I went to bed/the bed.

4) We drove to university/the university, opposite which was a temple.

5) Robert moved closer to the bed/bed.

6) People get sent to the prison/prison for that sort of thing.

7) How are we going to get from the church/church to the reception?

8) I wanted to go to university/the university but I wanted to be an actor more.

# Exercises: 6 Article use with certain groups of words

## Exercise 5 (section 6.6)

In some of the sentences below both the noun groups that are underlined are possible. In others only one is correct. Put a ring around the ones that are correct. The first one, in which both noun groups are possible, has been done for you.

1) I'm thirsty; let's go to (a pub/the pub.)

2) Nowadays a hairdresser's/the hairdresser's is a place where both men and women can have a haircut.

3) Don't forget, you're going to the doctor's/a doctor's today.

4) I need some stamps; where can I find a post office/the post office?

5) Our fear of the dentist's/a dentist's starts when we are children.

6) It's such a small village; you wouldn't expect it to have a pub/the pub.

## Exercise 6 (section 6.7)

In the sentences below, only one of the underlined noun groups is appropriate. Cross out the one that is wrong. The first one has been done for you.

1) Can you play a guitar/the guitar?

2) I once played a guitar/the guitar which had only five strings.

3) She started learning a piano/the piano at the age of five.

4) I've always had a flute/the flute, ever since I was a child.

5) I'm afraid a violin/the violin is an instrument I never mastered.

## Exercise 7 (section 6.8)

Complete these sentences, putting 'a', 'an', or 'the' and a noun in the spaces provided. The first one has been done for you.

1) Gorillas can only be found deep inside ...... *the jungle* ...... .

2) Finland is ................................................ that is famous for its lakes.

3) Lions are often called 'kings of ................................................' although in fact they live on ................................................ .

4) Camels have been called 'ships of ................................................' .

5) I prefer living in ................................................. ; it's quieter than the town.

6) When we were kids we loved the beach so we used to spend all our

   holidays at ................................................. , but now we prefer

   ................................................. , especially the Alps.

## Exercise 8 (section 6.9)

Choose an appropriate noun group to complete the following sentences.
The first one has been done for you.

1) Vietnam is to ........*the south*........ of China.

2) Scotland is to ...................................... of England.

3) The Conservative Party is on ...................................... of British politics.

4) London is in ...................................... of England.

5) ...................................... is a term applied to Western Europe and North

   America.

6) In Britain, India and some other countries, you should drive on

   ...................................... , but in most of the world people drive on

   ...................................... .

## Exercise 9 (section 6.10)

In the sentences below, only one of the underlined noun groups is
appropriate. Cross out the one that is wrong. The first one has been done
for you.

1) Lithuanian borders were set up in the spring/~~a spring~~.

2) In a summer/summer it's hot but in winter/a winter it's very cold.

3) During a day/the day it was very hectic but at the night/night it was

   desolate.

4) What are you doing after lunch on Tuesday/a Tuesday?

5) Past/The past is forgotten.

6) It was summer/a summer of intense heat.

7) Air force relief flights continue in morning/the morning.

8) I did a lot of work in Hamburg in the eighties/eighties.

## Exercise 10 (section 6.11)

In some of the sentences below both the noun groups that are underlined
are possible. In others only one is correct. Put a ring around the ones that
are correct. The first one has been done for you.

1) Do you suffer from a malaria/(malaria)?

2) I get fed up when I have a cold/cold because my nose goes bright red.

3) What is the best treatment for flu/the flu?

4) I took some aspirin for a headache/headache.

5) Leukaemia is cancer/a cancer of the blood.

6) Don't sit in a draught or you'll catch a chill/chill.

7) She developed stomach cancer/the stomach cancer a month after the
   marriage broke up.

8) I hope I haven't caught hepatitis/a hepatitis.

## Exercise 11 (section 6.13)

In the sentences below, only one of the underlined noun groups is
appropriate. Cross out the one that is wrong. The first one has been done
for you.

1) After a while, Maria came in, her hair/the hair freshly combed.

2) Bess kissed her on her cheek/the cheek.

3) The Baron leaned forward and looked her in the face/her face.

4) He put his hand/the hand on the shoulder/her shoulder.

5) She leaned close to him, resting her cheek/the cheek against his.

6) She slipped her arm/the arm under his and gave him a nudge.

7) The General had a pistol in the hand/his hand.

8) I kicked him hard on the leg/his leg.

9) He could have shot me in the foot/my foot.

**Exercise 12** (section 6.14)

Look at the sentences below. Decide whether you can leave out 'the' where it is underlined in each sentence, and put 'yes' or 'no' in the spaces provided. The first one has been done for you.

1) He became the chairman of the company. ......*yes*..............

2) I was the manager for only six weeks before the company went bankrupt. ......................

3) Mrs Jacobs is the head of two departments. ......................

4) They made him the leader of the gang. ......................

5) I'm going to meet the director of the club. ......................

6) Mr J. Benn, the owner of the shop, made no comment. ......................

7) He's been the captain for the last six matches. ......................

8) They made the President sign the document. ......................

9) She was the Queen for only a hundred days. ......................

10) I was the best man at his wedding. ......................

**Exercise 13** (section 6.15)

Complete these statements about English grammar, using 'the' and an appropriate grammatical term. The first one has been done for you.

1) The word 'the' is called ..........*the definite article*.......... .

2) 'Children' is .............................................. of 'child'.

3) 'Can' is .............................................. in 'I can do it', but in 'I hate drinking lemonade from a can' it is .............................................. .

4) 'A' and 'an' are the two forms of .............................................. .

5) After 'news' you should use a verb in .............................................. ; for example, 'the news is interesting'.

6) 'Sang' is .............................................. of 'sing', and 'sung' is .............................................. .

# 7 Articles and proper nouns

## Exercise 1 (sections 7.2 and 7.3)

Look at the map of Scotland. Fill in the spaces in the text below with proper nouns according to the map. Sometimes you will need the definite article, sometimes no article. The first one has been done for you.

Scotland occupies the northern part of Great Britain. It is separated from Northern Ireland by (1)......*the North Channel*...... while

(2)......................................... form the border with England. It lies

between two large bodies of water: (3)......................................... to

the west and (4)......................................... to the east. Many islands

lie off its coast: to the north are (5)......................................... and

to the west are (6).............................. ; (7)..............................
and (8).............................. are large islands in this group.

The highest mountains are (9).............................. and
(10).............................. in (11).............................. .
Other notable ranges of mountains or hills are (12)..............................
in the south of the country and (13).............................. in the
north.

The principal rivers are (14).............................. ,
(15).............................. and (16).............................. ;
there are numerous lakes, or 'lochs' as they are called, for example
(17).............................. and (18).............................. .

The largest cities are (19).............................. , which lies on
(20).............................. , and (21).............................. ,
which is close to (22).............................. .

## Exercise 2 (sections 7.2 and 7.3)

Try to answer the following questions about geography, using 'the' where
appropriate. The first one has been done for you.

1) Of which country is Washington the capital? .......*The USA*..............

2) What oceans does the Panama Canal join? ..............................

   and ..............................

3) Which river flows through London? ..............................

4) What desert occupies much of northern Africa? ..............................

5) Which country has the largest population in the world?

   ..............................

6) What joins the Red Sea and the Mediterranean?

   ..............................

7) Which is the largest continent? ..............................

8) What separates Spain and Morocco? ..............................

9) In which mountain range is Everest? ..............................

**Exercise 3** (sections 7.4 and 7.5)

Look at the map of central London. Complete the sentences below with proper nouns according to the map, using 'the' where appropriate. The first one has been done for you.

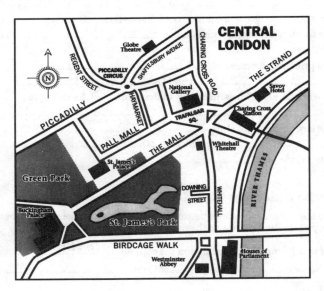

1) .......*The National Gallery*....................... is on Trafalgar Square.

2) ............................................................... are next to the River

Thames.

3) St James's Park lies between ...................................................................

and ......................................................... .

4) ............................................................... is situated on the Strand.

5) Buckingham Palace and Trafalgar Square are connected by

......................................................... .

6) St James's Palace lies at the end of ......................................................... .

7) ....................................... , ....................................... ,

....................................... and .......................................

are streets which radiate from Piccadilly Circus.

8) The Prime Minister's residence is in ........................................................ ,
   off Whitehall.

9) .................................................................... is between the Thames and
   the Strand.

10) .................................................................... runs north from Trafalgar
    Square.

11) The Whitehall is on .................................................................... .

## Exercise 4  (sections 7.7 and 7.8)

In the sentences below, only one of the underlined noun groups is
appropriate. Cross out the one that is wrong. The first one has been done
for you.

1) Italy won a World Cup/the World Cup in 1982.

2) Are you staying at home for Christmas/the Christmas?

3) Wimbledon/The Wimbledon is the most famous tennis event in the
   world.

4) Don't forget it's Mother's Day/the Mother's Day next week.

5) I can remember Easter/an Easter when it snowed all the time.

6) Olympic Games/The Olympic Games were restarted in Athens in 1896.

## Exercise 5  (section 7.9)

In the sentences below, only one of the underlined noun groups is
appropriate. Cross out the one that is wrong. The first one has been done
for you.

1) United Nations/The United Nations was formed in 1945.

2) ICI/The ICI is one of the world's largest companies.

3) John Major replaced Margaret Thatcher as leader of Conservative
   Party/the Conservative Party in 1990.

4) Cathay Pacific/The Cathay Pacific offers daily flights to Tokyo.

5) There have been arguments about the role of UNESCO/the UNESCO.

6) Several countries are interested in joining European Community/the
   European Community.

7) In 1954 he joined General Electric Company/the General Electric Company, or GEC/the GEC as it is usually known.

8) The Barclays Bank/Barclays Bank have opened a new branch in the High Street.

9) He's been a newsreader for BBC/the BBC for 10 years.

## Exercise 6 (section 7.10)

In the sentences below, only one of the underlined noun groups is appropriate. Cross out the one that is wrong. The first one has been done for you.

1) Newsweek/~~The Newsweek~~ appears, not surprisingly, every week.

2) Is Pravda/the Pravda a daily or a weekly newspaper?

3) The article was published in Spectator/the Spectator.

4) British newspapers are usually divided into popular papers, like Today/the Today and Sun/the Sun, and quality papers, like Guardian/the Guardian.

5) Times/The Times is a daily newspaper.

## Exercise 7 (section 7.11)

In the sentences below, only one of the underlined noun groups is appropriate. Cross out the one that is wrong. The first one has been done for you.

1) Whitehall/~~The Whitehall~~ has denied any knowledge of the affair.

2) The proposal was rejected by Finance Ministry/the Finance Ministry.

3) House of Lords/The House of Lords will vote on the bill tomorrow.

4) Kremlin/The Kremlin has so far made no response to the protest.

5) ... the state opening of Parliament/the Parliament by the Queen.

6) He was one of the youngest to be elected to Senate/the Senate.

**Exercise 8**  (section 7.13)

In the sentences below, only one of the underlined noun groups is appropriate. Cross out the one that is wrong. The first one has been done for you.

1) Can I introduce Janet Dunlop/~~the Janet Dunlop~~?

2) There's John Spence/a John Spence waiting to see you in the office.

3) Prince Philip/The Prince Philip is also known as Duke of Edinburgh/the Duke of Edinburgh.

4) Roosevelts/The Roosevelts have provided America with two presidents.

5) There's been Parkinson/a Parkinson in this village for generations.

6) 'Isn't that Richard Nixon over there?'- 'You mean, Richard Nixon/the Richard Nixon?'

7) Jones/The Jones and Smith/the Smith are two common British surnames.

8) Watermans/The Watermans? Oh yes, we know them well.

**Exercise 9**  (section 7.14)

Choose an expression from the list below to show what each sentence really refers to. (You will need to use some expressions more than once.) The first one has been done for you.

a product made by          a company like          a branch of          a copy of
a particular 'version' of          a person like          a work by

1) The London of the 21st century will be very different.
    ...... *a particular 'version' of* ...... London

2) Well, mine's a Hitachi.

    .................................................................. Hitachi

3) They've discovered a new Van Gogh.

    .................................................................. Van Gogh

4) They're opening a new McDonald's today.

    .................................................................. McDonald's

5) They're calling him the new Elvis.

    .................................................................. Elvis

103

6) I've just bought a Honda.

..................................................................... Honda

7) The Paris of my youth no longer exists.

..................................................................... Paris

8) We plan to be the IBM of the next century.

..................................................................... IBM

9) Have you got a Guardian that I could borrow?

..................................................................... the Guardian

# 8 Articles in the noun group

## Exercise 1 (section 8.3)

Look at each of the sentences below. If the sentence is still grammatically correct when you leave out the word 'of', put 'yes'. If the sentence is not correct when you leave out 'of', put 'no'. The first one has been done for you.

1) You can't fool everybody all of the time. ......*yes*........

2) Some of the answers have obviously been copied. .....................

3) The police have caught both of the thieves. .....................

4) Many of the crowd were waving flags. .....................

5) Two of the windows were broken. .....................

6) Half of the population didn't vote. .....................

## Exercise 2 (sections 8.2, 8.3 and 8.4)

Complete the following sentences, using the words in brackets and putting them into the right order. The first one has been done for you.

1) I have ......*many a*..................... fond memory of this place.
   (a/many)

2) There's no choice; ........................................... roads are blocked.
   (other/both/the)

3) You shouldn't ask ........................................... question. (a/such)

4) He wasted ........................................... chances that we gave him.
   (the/all/many)

5) I'm now earning ........................................... amount I used to.
   (five times/the)

6) It's ........................................... big challenge. (a/quite)

7) In fact, ........................................... people who came weren't
   invited. (few/the)

8) That's ........................................... thing we didn't want to
   happen. (one/the)

**Exercise 3** (section 8.6)

Look at the noun groups below and put a ring around the nouns which are being used as modifiers. The first one has been done for you.

1) a long (car) journey

2) the beautiful morning sunlight

3) an open kitchen window

4) a London fire brigade report

5) the British steel industry

6) the school medical officer

7) an expensive silk tie

8) a little wooden house

9) the strong Atlantic wind

10) an official government trade spokesman

11) a United Nations inspection team

12) a clothes shop

**Exercise 4** (section 8.7)

Complete the following sentences, using the words in brackets and putting them into the right order. The first one has been done for you.

1) Have you ever met ....._so stupid a boy_.....?

   (stupid/so/boy/a)

2) I don't think I've ever read ................................................................ .

   (a/such/essay/brilliant)

3) It was just ................................................ to miss.

   (too/a/chance/good)

4) Do you realise ................................................ it is?

   (a/what/difficult/task)

5) I just don't know ................................................ that is.

   (possibility/likely/a/how)

6) We mustn't ignore ................................................ as this.

   (a/serious/as/threat)

## Exercise 5 (section 8.8)

The sentences below are correct as they are. However, some of the underlined articles can be left out. Put a ring around these optional articles. The first one has been done for you.

1) In some cases you can use a definite or (an) indefinite article.

2) This will affect the normal relationship between a husband and a wife.

3) We bought a television and a vacuum cleaner.

4) Storms affected the north and the west of the country.

5) He has a brother and a sister.

6) The mother and the baby are doing well.

7) We ought to clear up this mess. Give me a dustpan and a brush.

8) The path led across the hills and the valleys of the county.

9) You'll need a knife and a fork to eat that.

## Exercise 6 (section 8.9)

Complete each of the sentences below. Use the definite article together with the most appropriate adjective from the list. Use each adjective only once. The first one has been done for you.

| bizarre | impossible | obvious | unexpected |
|---------|------------|---------------|------------|
| exotic | inevitable | supernatural | unknown |

1) Kawaguchi's behaviour, always erratic, now bordered on
   ...... *the bizarre* ...... .

2) 'So Vesco had a gun,' said Martello, stating ................................................ .

3) I think he has a taste for ........................................................ .

4) They had driven off into ........................................................ , towards a

   place that officially did not exist.

5) No one can achieve ........................................................ .

6) They were interested in ........................................................ and looking

   for UFOs.

7) Expect ........................................................ .

8) Nature always seems cruel and heartless when we are faced with

   ........................................................: death.

## Exercise 7 (section 8.10)

Make seven complete (and sensible!) sentences by matching the beginning of each one on the left with the most appropriate ending on the right. The first one has been done for you.

1) The slower you eat, ———

2) The further it is from the sun,

3) The wider your circle of friends,

4) The stronger the walls of a horse's foot,

5) The larger the biscuit,

6) The lower the power of the satellite signal,

7) The more intense the exercise,

a) the greater the likelihood of meeting someone with whom you have a lot in common.

b) the shorter the length of time you'll be able to keep doing it.

c) the longer the baking time.

d) the more you will think you have eaten.

e) the slower it travels.

f) the fewer the nails needed to hold the shoe in place.

g) the larger the dish diameter required.

# Answer Key

## Chapter 1

### Exercise 1

/ðə/: 2, 5, 6, 7, 8, 11, 12, 13, 14
/ðiː/: 1, 3, 4, 9, 10

### Exercise 2

1) an
2) a, an
3) A, an
4) a, a, an
5) a
6) An, a

### Exercise 3

Pronounced with an initial
consonant sound; use 'the'
/ðə/ or 'a' /ə/:
BBC, finger, hand, head, leg,
neck, nose, one-man band,
toe, UK, uniform, unit,
university, useful idea

Pronounced with an initial
vowel sound; use 'the' /ðiː/ or
'an' /ən/:
arm, ear, eye, FBI agent,
honest man, honour, MP, ugly
man, umbrella, uncle

### Exercise 4

1) The /ðə/ b - a /ə/ d.
   (daughter)
2) The /ðiː/ l - an /ən/ h.
   (father)
3) The /ðiː/ m - an /ən/ s.
   (sister)
4) The /ðiː/ x - a /ə/ u.
   (cousin)
5) The /ðə/ y - a /ə/ w.
   (nephew)
6) The /ðiː/ i - an /ən/ o.
   (grandson)
7) The /ðə/ g - an /ən/ a.
   (aunt)
8) The /ðiː/ f - a /ə/ p.
   (parents)
9) The /ðə/ t - an /ən/ e.
   (niece)
10) The /ðiː/ n - an /ən/ r.
    (mother)

## Chapter 2

### Exercise 1

1) a
2) –
3) a
4) –
5) –
6) an
7) a
8) –
9) –
10) –
11) a
12) –
13) a
14) –
15) –
16) a
17) –
18) –
19) –
20) –

### Exercise 2

1) plural
2) plural
3) 'dresses' - count
   'trousers' - plural
4) plural
5) plural
6) 'glasses' - plural
   'gloves' - count
7) plural
8) plural

### Exercise 3

1) type
2) type
3) unit
4) unit
5) type
6) type
7) unit
8) type
9) unit
10) type

### Exercise 4

1) yes
2) no
3) yes
4) yes
5) no
6) yes
7) no
8) yes
9) no
10) no
11) yes
12) no

### Exercise 5

1) cheeses
2) woods
3) metals
4) wines
5) beers

### Exercise 6

1) vehicle
2) bird
3) insect
4) dog
5) cat
6) flower

### Exercise 7

1) memory
2) study
3) a reason
4) a rubber
5) a faith
6) a memory
7) rubber
8) faith
9) a study
10) reason

### Exercise 8

1) an iron
2) Language
3) a beauty
4) experience
5) a tin
6) work
7) law
8) a speech
9) Play
10) Charity

### Exercise 9

1) a drop of
2) a lump of
3) a piece of/a lump of
4) a pair of
5) a piece of
6) a piece of/an item of
7) a pair of
8) a piece of

# Answer Key

9) a grain of
10) a piece of/an item of
11) a piece of/an item of
12) a grain of

# Chapter 3

## Exercise 1

1) one
2) it
3) one
4) it
5) it
6) one
7) one

## Exercise 2

1) a playwright
2) a composer
3) a scientist
4) a film star
5) a cartoon character
6) an explorer
7) an artist
8) a philosopher
9) a writer

## Exercise 3

1) yes
2) no
3) no
4) yes
5) no
6) no
7) no
8) yes
9) no
10) yes, yes, yes

## Exercise 4

1) 40p a kilo
2) 600 miles an hour
3) $2,500 a month
4) twice a week
5) 8 hours a day
6) 80 kilometres an hour

# Chapter 4

## Exercise 1

1) a
2) a
3) a
4) the
5) the
6) a
7) The
8) a
9) a

10) the
11) a
12) the
13) a
14) the
15) the

## Exercise 2

1) eggs
2) milk
3) butter
4) the butter
5) it
6) the milk
7) it/the butter
8) the eggs
9) them

## Exercise 3

1) same
2) different
3) same
4) same
5) different
6) same

## Exercise 4

1) the shelves
2) the answer
3) the students/the pupils
4) the stairs/the steps
5) the questions
6) the pages
7) The heels
8) the tyres
9) The price
10) the picture

## Exercise 5

the floor, the wall, the windows, the light, the door

## Exercise 6

1) e
2) j
3) g
4) f
5) c
6) b
7) i
8) a
9) h
10) d

## Exercise 7

1) the police station
2) the railway station
3) the hospital
4) the theatre, the cinema

5) the post office, a church
6) the park

## Exercise 8

1) the
2) a
3) The, the
4) a
5) a
6) –/the
7) the, the
8) an
9) the
10) the

## Exercise 9

1) the
2) The
3) a
4) the
5) a
6) the
7) a
8) the
9) a
10) the

## Exercise 10

1) the arrival of the stars
2) The opening of the shop
3) the disappearance of a boy
4) the loss of all his money
5) the birth of a baby girl
6) the existence of the painting
7) the destruction of the city
8) the discovery of the body
9) The defeat of the rebels

## Exercise 11

1) the largest
2) the hardest
3) the highest
4) the longest
5) The heaviest
6) the nearest, the closest
7) The oldest

## Exercise 12

1) the first
2) the wrong, the right
3) the same
4) The next/The first
5) the only
6) a right
7) the last
8) the same
9) a last
10) the last

# Chapter 5

## Exercise 1
1) generic
2) particular
3) generic
4) particular
5) particular
6) generic
7) generic

## Exercise 2
1) A kitchen
2) A bridge
3) An umbrella
4) A church
5) An egg
6) A university
7) A dictionary
8) A market
9) A thief
10) A bomb

## Exercise 3
1) the giraffe
2) the whale
3) the lion
4) the gorilla
5) the elephant
6) the camel
7) the dog

## Exercise 4
1) the heart
2) the bedroom, the living-room
3) the child
4) The doctor
5) The telephone
6) the classroom, the teacher, the learner/the student/the pupil

## Exercise 5
1) cars
2) the heart
3) A writer/The writer
4) the wheel
5) A tortoise
6) whales/the whale
7) A chair

## Exercise 6
1) The English
2) The Germans
3) The Chinese
4) The Greeks
5) The Russians

## Exercise 7
1) The unemployed
2) The healthy
3) The lame
4) The rich
5) The blind
6) The poor
7) The deaf
8) The uneducated
9) The hungry
10) The homeless

# Chapter 6

## Exercise 1
1) the radio
2) television/the television
3) a newspaper
4) the radio
5) a telephone/a phone
6) a television
7) the post
8) the phone/the telephone
9) the papers/the newspaper

## Exercise 2
1) The train
2) the ferry
3) the boat
4) the bus
5) the underground, a bus, a taxi

## Exercise 3
1) ballet
2) the theatre
3) television
4) a cinema
5) the opera
6) Film
7) the movies

## Exercise 4
1) the hospital
2) church
3) bed
4) the university
5) the bed
6) prison
7) the church
8) university

## Exercise 5
1) a pub/the pub
2) a hairdresser's/the hairdresser's
3) the doctor's
4) a post office/the post office
5) the dentist's
6) a pub

## Exercise 6
1) the guitar
2) a guitar
3) the piano
4) a flute
5) the violin

## Exercise 7
1) the jungle
2) a country
3) the jungle, the plains
4) the desert
5) the country
6) the seaside, the mountains

## Exercise 8
1) the south
2) the north
3) the right
4) the south-east/the south
5) The West
6) the left, the right

## Exercise 9
1) the spring
2) summer, winter
3) the day, night
4) Tuesday
5) The past
6) a summer
7) the morning
8) the eighties

## Exercise 10
1) malaria
2) a cold
3) flu/the flu
4) a headache
5) cancer/a cancer
6) a chill
7) stomach cancer
8) hepatitis

## Exercise 11
1) her hair
2) the cheek
3) the face
4) his hand, her shoulder

# Answer Key

5) her cheek
6) her arm
7) his hand
8) the leg
9) the foot

## Exercise 12

1) yes
2) yes
3) yes
4) yes
5) no
6) yes
7) yes
8) no
9) yes
10) yes

## Exercise 13

1) the definite article
2) the plural (form)
3) a verb/a modal, a noun
4) the indefinite article
5) the (third person) singular
6) the past tense/the simple past, the past participle

# Chapter 7

## Exercise 1

1) the North Channel
2) the Cheviot Hills
3) the Atlantic (Ocean)
4) the North Sea
5) the Orkney Islands/the Orkneys
6) the Hebrides
7), 8) Mull, Skye
9), 10) Ben Nevis, Ben Macdui
11) the Grampian Mountains/the Grampians
12) the Southern Uplands
13) the North-West Highlands
14), 15), 16) the Tay, the Spey, the Clyde
17), 18) Loch Ness, Loch Lomond
19) Glasgow
20) the Clyde
21) Edinburgh
22) the Firth of Forth

## Exercise 2

1) The USA
2) The Pacific (Ocean), the Atlantic (Ocean)
3) The Thames
4) The Sahara (Desert)

5) China/The People's Republic of China
6) The Suez Canal
7) Asia
8) The Straits of Gibraltar/The Mediterranean (Sea)
9) The Himalayas

## Exercise 3

1) The National Gallery
2) The Houses of Parliament
3) the Mall, Birdcage Walk
4) The Savoy Hotel
5) the Mall
6) Pall Mall
7) Piccadilly, Regent Street, Shaftesbury Avenue, Haymarket
8) Downing Street
9) Charing Cross Station
10) Charing Cross Road
11) Whitehall

## Exercise 4

1) the World Cup
2) Christmas
3) Wimbledon
4) Mother's Day
5) an Easter
6) The Olympic Games

## Exercise 5

1) The United Nations
2) ICI
3) the Conservative Party
4) Cathay Pacific
5) UNESCO
6) the European Community
7) the General Electric Company, GEC
8) Barclays Bank
9) the BBC

## Exercise 6

1) Newsweek
2) Pravda
3) the Spectator
4) Today, the Sun, the Guardian
5) The Times

## Exercise 7

1) Whitehall
2) the Finance Ministry
3) The House of Lords
4) The Kremlin
5) Parliament
6) the Senate

## Exercise 8

1) Janet Dunlop
2) a John Spence
3) Prince Philip, the Duke of Edinburgh
4) The Roosevelts
5) a Parkinson
6) the Richard Nixon
7) Jones, Smith
8) The Watermans

## Exercise 9

1) a particular 'version' of
2) a product made by
3) a work by
4) a branch of
5) a person like
6) a product made by
7) a particular 'version' of
8) a company like
9) a copy of

# Chapter 8

## Exercise 1

1) yes
2) no
3) yes
4) no
5) no
6) yes

## Exercise 2

1) many a
2) both the other
3) such a
4) all the many
5) five times the
6) quite a
7) the few
8) the one

## Exercise 3

1) car
2) morning
3) kitchen
4) London, fire brigade
5) steel
6) school
7) silk
8) –
9) Atlantic
10) government, trade
11) United Nations, inspection
12) clothes

## Exercise 4

1) so stupid a boy
2) such a brilliant essay
3) too good a chance
4) what a difficult task
5) how likely a possibility
6) as serious a threat/a threat as serious

## Exercise 5

In the following sentences, the articles which are optional have been left out.

1) In some cases you can use a definite or indefinite article.
2) This will affect the normal relationship between husband and wife.

3) We bought a television and a vacuum cleaner.
4) Storms affected the north and west of the country.
5) He has a brother and sister.
6) Mother and baby are doing well.
7) We ought to clear up this mess. Give me a dustpan and brush.
8) The path led across the hills and valleys of the county.
9) You'll need a knife and fork to eat that.

## Exercise 6

1) the bizarre
2) the obvious
3) the exotic
4) the unknown
5) the impossible
6) the supernatural
7) the unexpected
8) the inevitable

## Exercise 7

1) d
2) e
3) a
4) f
5) c
6) g
7) b

# Index

Items in **bold** are technical terms. Items in roman are categories of words that are discussed in the text. Items in *italic* are lexical words that are discussed in the text or are included in the lists. Numbers refer to the chapter and section.

114